J.K.M. AUCHINLECK.
Jeni Wood.
14:1:59:

EPITAPH FOR GEORGE DILLON

by John Osborne

*

THE ENTERTAINER
LOOK BACK IN ANGER

EPITAPH
FOR
GEORGE DILLON

A Play in Three Acts

by

JOHN OSBORNE

AND

ANTHONY CREIGHTON

FABER AND FABER

24 Russell Square

London

First published in mcmlviii
by Faber and Faber Limited
24 Russell Square London W.C.1
Printed in Great Britain by
Latimer Trend & Co Ltd Plymouth

TO E.M.C.
WITH OUR LOVE

NOTE

The first professional performance in Great Britain of EPITAPH FOR GEORGE DILLON was given at the Royal Court Theatre, Sloane Square, London, on 11th February 1958 by the English Stage Company. It was directed by William Gaskill and the décor was by Stephen Doncaster. The cast was as follows:

JOSIE ELLIOT	Wendy Craig
RUTH GRAY	Yvonne Mitchell
MRS. ELLIOT	Alison Leggatt
NORAH ELLIOT	Avril Elgar
PERCY ELLIOT	Toke Townley
GEORGE DILLON	Robert Stephens
GEOFFREY COLWYN-STUART	Philip Locke
MR. WEBB	Paul Bailey
BARNEY EVANS	Nigel Davenport

All professional inquiries in regard to this play should be addressed to the author's agent, Margery Vosper Ltd., 32 Shaftesbury Avenue, London W.1, and all amateur inquiries should be addressed to Messrs. Evans Brothers Ltd., Montague House, Russell Square, London W.C.1.

cast in order of appearance

JOSIE ELLIOT
RUTH GRAY
MRS. ELLIOT
NORAH ELLIOT
PERCY ELLIOT
GEORGE DILLON
GEOFFREY COLWYN-STUART
MR. WEBB
BARNEY EVANS

The action of the play takes place in the home of the Elliot family just outside London.

ACT I

The home of the Elliot family, just outside London. Spring, late afternoon.

The action takes place in the sitting-room and hall. The front door being stage right. In the hall, immediately facing, are the stairs which turn off left. Flat against the staircase is a hat and coat stand, shelving hats, coats, magazines, umbrellas, etc., in the midst of which is a vase of everlasting flowers. Upstage of the hall, under the arch formed by the stairs is the door leading into the room called the lounge. Next to this upstage, is the invisible wall which divides the hall from the sitting-room. The only object suggesting the wall is a door set upstage. Downstage of this, set against the "wall" facing into the sitting-room is a radiogram, upon which stands a biscuit barrel and a silver-plated dish containing wax or real fruit. Nearby an arm-chair of the "contemporary" kind faces downstage. Against the upstage wall, right, is a dining-chair. Centre, an ornate cocktail cabinet and another dining-chair. On the wall, flanking this, are two wall lights, in the centre of which is painted a group of wild ducks, in flight.

Left centre is the door leading to the kitchen, next to which is the kitchen hatch, which when raised, reveals the kitchen beyond. Below the hatch is a tea-trolley. Above the hatch, on the wall, is a tinted photograph of a wedding group. In the stage left wall, french windows which look out on to a small back garden. Below the french windows, a half-round occasional table, above hangs a mirror. In front of the french windows a settee, again of the utility-contemporary period. At the head a white-painted wrought-iron floor lamp. Upstage, left centre, a draw-leaf table with dining-chair and arm dining-chair in position. On the cocktail cabinet stands a large china model of an alsatian dog, and a photograph of a soldier in a silver frame, decorated with "Haig" poppies.

11

AT RISE OF CURTAIN, JOSIE *is on stage alone. She is about twenty, pretty in a hard, frilly way and nobody's fool. At the moment she is not looking her best. The turban she is wearing reveals a couple of curlers above her forehead, her jumper is grubby and her slacks baggy, stained and not very fetching. She is sprawled in the armchair. In a vicious idleness she stares at a highly coloured weekly. Mozart is on the radio, delicate, liquid. She flips through the magazine, is about to put it down when something catches her attention. She reads.*

JOSIE: Fancy writing up and asking *that*!
(*She laughs and goes on with her reading, fondling one of her curlers as she does so. Presently she throws the magazine down.*)
Soppy cow!
(*She sighs and leans back, thrusts her hands into the top of her slacks, rubbing her stomach and frowning. She gets up and stares at her reflection in the mirror. Pursing her lips experimentally, she watches the effect. She leans forward and tries fluffing up her eyebrows. It doesn't seem very successful and she sighs again.*)
Oh, that damn row!
(*She goes to the radio, stabs at the knobs, then gives up and switches it off. Her eye catches the magazine again and she goes through it again until she finds what she is looking for. She stares at it sullenly and flings the paper on the floor. At the mirror again she tries several grimaces, puts out her tongue. A little more speculation, and she goes over to the settee, and sinks down on her knees. She stretches, and, catching sight of the resulting white space between her jumper and slacks, strokes herself dreamily. She slides forward on to her stomach, her hands moving over the arm of the settee, curiosity in her fingers and boredom in her body. She starts to sing, in a studied, offhand way, one of those downward-inflection popular hits.*)
"Why don't you Give Me . . . Give Me. . . ."
(*Pause.*)

12

"All that you have to share.
Why don't you Give Me . . . Give me. . . ."
(*She picks her nose daintily, and turns over on her back.*)
"And tell me you really c-are. . . ."
(*Her hand trails the space beside her, like a hand in rippling water, then stops, as she says deliberately:*)
I wonder—what it *would* be like?
(*She is about to swing her legs above her head, when the front door bell rings.*)
Good-O!
(*She rushes off to the front door, almost reaches it, when she remembers something, and comes back into the dining-room. Her eyes light on her handbag, and she snatches it up, taking it with her, through the hall, straight to the front door. The bell is still ringing, and she calls out:*)
Oh, all right! Wait a minute! Wait a minute! (*Opens front door.*)
(*We hear a voice saying:*) "Parcel for Mrs. Elliot. Three pounds fifteen and ninepence to pay."
Miss Elliot, if you please. I thought you were never coming. Here you are. You have been a long time. I thought you'd have been here this morning. I haven't even been able to go up the road, waiting for you to come. What? I haven't got it. Well, you'll have to change it.
(*A few minutes of change fumbling before she slams the front door, and goes into the sitting-room with a square cardboard box in her arms, which she starts to open excitedly, kneeling on the floor. Off comes the string and paper, then the lid and a layer of tissue paper. She rises quickly, places the box on the settee, takes a cigarette from her handbag, which she puts in her mouth, kicks off her slippers, and goes to the radiogram, unzipping her slacks at the same time. She raises the lid, switches it on, and takes off her slacks, leaving them on the floor, one leg inside out. She selects a record*

13

from the pile beside her, and puts it on. Cigarette in mouth, she waits expectantly until the corncrake growl of a New Orleans trumpet strides off into a piece of fairly traditional jazz. She runs back to her parcel and takes out the contents, in a scurry of paper and impatience, which turn out to be a pair of black, tapering trousers. She puts them on, zipping up the sides with a little difficulty. Hands on hips, she looks down at the result anxiously, then delightedly. She goes nearer to the mirror, to get a better view of herself. She bounces up and down, looking at this angle and that, patting her stomach, feeling the seat until she is finally satisfied. She lights her cigarette, then, putting her hands in her unfamiliar pockets, strikes a more or less elegant attitude and a bored expression, one black undeniably slim leg straight out in front of the other. She inclines her head back, and blows out a cloud of smoke. JOSIE may be funny at times, but she is never consciously so. She begins to dance, slowly at first, and surprisingly well, across R., ending up by lying with her back on the floor, and her knees up. The front door opens, and RUTH enters hall. JOSIE sits up quickly.)

That you, Mum?

(RUTH closes the door, but makes no reply. JOSIE takes off her new trousers, and starts slipping them back in their box. As she is doing this, RUTH enters from the hall. She is about forty, slim, smartly dressed, attractive. She carries a small week-end case, which she puts down when she gets into the sitting-room.)

You're in early.

(RUTH goes to the radiogram, and switches it off.)

RUTH: Do you mind if we do without New Orleans just for the moment?

(She crosses and picks up JOSIE'S old slacks from the floor.)

Are you looking for these?

(She throws them over, and JOSIE manages to catch them.)

14

JOSIE: Thought you were Mum.

RUTH: I don't suppose you'd made any tea?

JOSIE: (*putting on her slacks*). I had some at dinner time.
(RUTH *goes into the kitchen, and puts the kettle on to boil.*)
You're in early.

RUTH: (*off*). Why aren't you at work today?

JOSIE: Wasn't feeling very good this morning.

RUTH: (*off*). Oh?

JOSIE: So Mum said I'd better stay indoors.
(*She is staring at the case* RUTH *has left on the floor.*)
Going on your holidays?

RUTH: (*off*). No—coming back. Satisfied?

JOSIE: How can you be coming back, when you haven't
been away? Anyway, I haven't had a day off work
for ages—it won't hurt them. (*Picking up the case to
see if it is empty.*) New case?

RUTH: (*off*). I picked it up from where I left it last night—
at Leicester Square Left Luggage Office. And it's full
of obscene photographs.

JOSIE: Oh?

RUTH: (*appearing in the doorway*). Josie: give me a cigarette,
will you? I came all the way back in the train without
one. (*Back into kitchen.*) There wasn't any post for
me was there?

JOSIE: (*crossing to her handbag* R.). Package came for you—
registered.

RUTH: (*off*). No letters?

JOSIE: Just the pools. It's only a small one. Doesn't weigh
anything hardly.

RUTH: (*off*). And what's inside it?

JOSIE: (*searching in her handbag*). How should I know?

RUTH: (*off*). Didn't you open it?

JOSIE: What do you mean? Course I didn't open it.

RUTH: (*coming back in*). If you must fry yourself food when
you're feeling ill, you might have the decency to clear
up afterwards. The gas stove is covered in grease and
muck—it's filthy.

(*She takes off her hat, and moves to the occasional table down* L., *where she sees a small package.*)
Is this it? (*Examines it, and goes on, rather absently.*)
You've even left the breakfast things in the sink.
(JOSIE *is holding her packet of cigarettes, watching her curiously.* RUTH *stares at the packet.*)

JOSIE: Typewritten.

RUTH: You've had damn-all to do all day. It's like a slum when your mother comes in.

JOSIE: Aren't you going to open it?

RUTH: (*a quick glance at her*). I said you're a slut.

JOSIE: Oh, did you? I didn't hear.
(*After a momentary hesitation,* RUTH *unwraps the package.* JOSIE *slips her cigarettes back into her handbag, and moves over to the kitchen door. From a small cardboard box,* RUTH *takes out a man's wrist watch.* JOSIE *takes it in, and goes into the kitchen.*)

JOSIE: I'll get a cup of tea.
(*The watch is lying in* RUTH'S *hand, as with the other, she takes out a piece of notepaper, and reads it. Then she places the box on the table. She stares at the paper, stroking her temples with her fingers, as if she felt a weight in her head. Presently, she calls out to* JOSIE *in the kitchen. The edge has gone out of her voice, and she sounds tired.*)

RUTH: Josie: be a good girl and get me that cigarette, will you?
(JOSIE *enters with a cup of tea, which she hands to her.*)

JOSIE: That man was here again this afternoon, asking for you.

RUTH: I've asked you twice to let me have one of your cigarettes. Please! I'll pay you back tonight.

JOSIE: Haven't got one. Sorry.

RUTH: (*turning back to the table*). Oh well, I suppose I'll have to go upstairs, anyway. There may be some in the bedroom somewhere.
(*She replaces the watch and note in the little box.*)
Who was here, did you say?

16

JOSIE: That man. I don't know who he is. The one who came on Saturday, and again the other day. That's the third time he's been.

RUTH: I thought you told him I didn't get in till 5.30?

JOSIE: I did. He said he'd come back one evening.

RUTH: (*to arm-chair and sitting*). Well, what time did he come today?

JOSIE: About four, I suppose.

RUTH: He doesn't sound very bright, whoever he is. What's he look like?

JOSIE: Not bad. Bit like Frankie Vaughan.

RUTH: Who the hell's Frankie Vaughan. (*Sipping tea.*) You make a putrid cup of tea, don't you. Doesn't he say what he wants?

JOSIE: Just that he wants to see you—that's all.

RUTH: Strange way to go about it. Calling at the time when you've specifically told him I shall be out. You didn't tell him anything did you?

JOSIE: Tell him what? That he looked like Frankie Vaughan?

RUTH: Oh, Josie, for heaven's sake, can't you see I'm tired? All I want is a cigarette and a bath.

(*The front door opens and* MRS. ELLIOT *comes in. She is a sincere, emotionally restrained little woman in her early fifties, who firmly believes that every cloud has a silver lining. She carries various carrier-bags filled with shopping. At the hall-stand she removes her coat.*)

RUTH: That's your mother. For heaven's sake make a start on that kitchen so that she can get started on the supper without having to clear up your mess first.

JOSIE: (*moving to kitchen*). O.K.

MRS. E.: Are you there, Josie? (*Taking off hat.*)

JOSIE: Hullo, Mum. You're not in any trouble are you, Auntie?

RUTH: In trouble? Do you mean in the general or the popular sense?

JOSIE: What?

MRS. E.: (*coming into sitting-room with bags*). Hullo, dear, hullo Josie. Managed to get a seat on the train today, thank goodness. (*Into kitchen.*)

RUTH: Hullo Kate.

JOSIE: Hullo mum.

MRS. E.: Oh Josie, you are a naughty girl, you really are. (*Into sitting-room.*) I was hoping you'd have everything nice and clean and tidy when I came in.

JOSIE: I was just going to do it.

MRS. E.: Just look at it out there. It would be tonight too, when there's so much to do.

RUTH: Here, let me take that from you. (*Taking one of the bags.*)

MRS. E.: Thank you, Ruth.

JOSIE: I'm sorry, Mum. Auntie Ruth was talking to me just as I was going to do it. Everyone seems a bit early tonight. (*Into kitchen.*)

MRS. E.: (*unpacking carrier*). I asked Mr. Beamish to let me off five minutes early. Didn't like it either. I thought I'd just miss the rush. Funny what a difference a few minutes makes. Anyway, I managed to get some shopping up the road before they closed. Oh dear, what a rush. There we are. You're back early, Ruth dear. Weren't you feeling well? Wonder if George likes parsley sauce.

RUTH: It wasn't anything. Central heating in the office, I expect.

MRS. E.: Well—Josie complained she wasn't too great this morning at breakfast time, so I made her stay at home. I hope you haven't gone and caught something off of her—food poisoning or something.

RUTH: Yes.

MRS. E.: You do look tired, I must say.

RUTH: Oh, I'm better now. Josie gave her *Auntie* a cup of tea.

MRS. E.: You always hate her calling you Auntie don't you. What can you expect dear when that's what you are? Now, I wanted you to do something for me. What was it? Josie, don't bother with those things now.

18

Lay the table for me in here instead, there's a good girl.

RUTH: You seem a bit overloaded.

MRS. E.: Well, I had to get a few extras.

JOSIE: (*in from kitchen*). Where's the fire, Mum?

MRS. E.: Now try and help me a little, Josie. I'm rather cross with you over that kitchen, my girl.

JOSIE: Well, I'm doing it, aren't I?

RUTH: All right you two, I'll help, only don't go on about it, please. (*Into kitchen.*)

JOSIE: Well, she was "going on" a bit herself just now.

MRS. E.: That's enough, Josie. (*Clearing table.*) I had hoped that at least you could have had the table laid.

JOSIE: Yes, Mum, all right.

MRS. E.: I'm in such a muddle, I don't know where I am. I haven't a chance to do a thing. Hope your father comes in on time.

JOSIE: What's all the panic? Don't tell me you've got somebody coming?

MRS. E.: Yes, I have.

JOSIE: Who on earth is it?

(RUTH *comes in with loaded tray, puts it down and she and* MRS. E. *start laying the table.*)

MRS. E.: Young George is coming, that's all.

RUTH: George?

MRS. E.: George Dillon. The young fellow that works at my place. You know. I told you about him.

RUTH: Oh, did you. I don't remember.

JOSIE: Oh, him. (*She yawns loudly and flops into the arm-chair.*)

MRS. E.: Of course I told you. I've often spoken about him. I've asked him down to tea lots of times. But each time some appointment seems to turn up and he can't come. Well, he's coming now, for certain. He's a very busy chap. Always on the go.

RUTH: Oh, that one. The rather superior young man who's so much younger than the rest of you. Is he still there? I thought you said the job wasn't quite good

19

enough for him.

MRS. E.: I've always felt a bit sorry for him, that's all. He seemed so much on his own all the time. And, one day, I started telling him about our Raymond, and he was most interested. He was in the services as well, you see.

RUTH: Quite a coincidence.

MRS. E.: Yes. He went right through the war.

RUTH: I had the idea we all did.

(*Pause.*)

MRS. E.: No, Ruth, some boys didn't get to see the end of it.

RUTH: I'm sorry, Kate. I've had a bit of a day, I'm afraid. I'm not in the right frame of mind to talk to young men, refined or not. If I can't do anything for you down here, I'll go and run myself a bath, if you don't mind.

MRS. E.: Oh! Were you going to have a bath now?

RUTH: Yes. Why?

MRS. E.: Well, I can't go into a long rigamarole now—I've too much to do before George comes. But you see— well, you've got to know sometime, I suppose—I've asked him to stay.

JOSIE: Stay? What, here?

MRS. E.: It won't be for long—just till he finds somewhere else to go.

JOSIE: What's wrong with where he is?

MRS. E.: He's not very happy there. I'll tell you later. Don't worry me with a lot of questions now, Josie. There's too much to do.

RUTH: Well, it's your business. It's your house—not mine. What about Percy?

MRS. E.: Nothing about Percy. It's got nothing to do with him.

RUTH: You're right, of course. (*Rather dryly.*) It isn't his house, either.

MRS. E.: There's just one thing——

JOSIE: There won't half be an atmosphere when he finds out. You know what Dad's like—he hasn't got over those budgerigars you bought yet.

20

MRS. E.: He knows what he can do, and it won't take me long
to tell him. Oh, do clear up that paper and stuff,
Josie. The place looks awful. What was I saying?

RUTH: "There's just one thing."

MRS. E.: Oh yes, Ruth. I was going to ask if you would mind
very much moving out of your room for a few days,
and going in with Norah.

RUTH: Why yes, I do mind. Is it really necessary? Does
George Whats-his-name have to have my room?

MRS. E.: No, he doesn't have to, but I thought it would be
nicer—being Ray's old room, he'd like it. More like
a man's room. Still——

RUTH: (*quietly*). You know, I do like to have at least some
time to myself. And anyway, Norah sleeps with her
mouth open.

MRS. E.: Oh, very well, Ruth. Josie can go in with her. You
won't mind, will you, Josie?

JOSIE: (*folding up paper*). Oh, all right. All this blessed fuss!
(*Into kitchen.*)

RUTH: I'm sorry, Kate, but you do understand.

MRS. E.: Never mind. I just thought it would be nicer, that's
all. It doesn't matter, dear. And there's no fuss,
Madame Josie, thank you. God pays debts without
money, I always say.

RUTH: You haven't any aspirin, have you? I don't seem to
know where any of my things are——

MRS. E.: There are some in the medicine chest, I think. And if
you're going up, would you mind getting some of
Josie's stuff into Norah's room—as that's going to be
the arrangement?

RUTH: Right.
(*She is lost in her own thoughts and does not move.*
MRS. E. *is too preoccupied to notice.*)
(*Pause.*)

MRS. E.: Only would you mind doing it now, while Josie and
I get straight down here? George'll be here very soon
—he's only got to pick up his bag from his digs. Is that
your case?

21

RUTH: (*picking it up, and into hall*). I'll take it up with me. (*Taking off scarf and hanging it up.*) Is there anything else?

MRS. E.: No, thank you very much, Ruth. I must get started now.

(RUTH *goes upstairs.*)

Oh, yes—(*into hall*)—Ruth, dear, would you put a clean towel in the bathroom for George? I expect he'd like a wash when he comes in.

RUTH: (*halfway upstairs*). Yes.

MRS. E.: I'm sorry you're not feeling well, dear.

(RUTH *goes on upstairs.* MRS. E. *returns to sitting-room.*)

MRS. E.: Now, where are we?

(*The table by now is almost laid, and* MRS. E. *completes it.*)

JOSIE: (*in from kitchen*). Will it be the boiled pork, Mum? There isn't much left—least, not after Dad gets his hands on it.

MRS. E.: He can have it all, as far as I'm concerned. Anyway, it won't worry George, he's a vegetarian. (*To cocktail cabinet.*)

JOSIE: A what?

MRS. E.: (*triumphantly*). A vegetarian. Now, where's the sherry got to, I wonder? Oh, yes.

(*She finds the bottle, and puts it on the table.*)

JOSIE: Oh, one of them. He sounds a bit wishy-washy to me.

MRS. E.: Well, he's not—he's a real gentleman.

JOSIE: That's what I mean. My, we are going posh, aren't we? Sherry! Anybody'd think it was Christmas.

MRS. E.: (*to kitchen*). That's enough of that, young lady. Now go and get dressed and make yourself a bit more presentable, or else George will think I brought you up in the slums.

JOSIE: (*idly round the room*). George, George, George. Georgie Porgie puddeny-pie, kissed the girls and made them cry——

MRS. E.: (*from kitchen*). Now do as I say, dear, please.

JOSIE: All right, Mum. (*She starts to sing.*)

"Why don't you Give Me . . .
         Give Me. Give Me . . .
         All that you——"
"All that you
         Have to share . . ."

(*Her eyes light on the small package on the table down* L. *She moves over to it.*)

(*She extracts the note from the package, and unfolds it.*)

MRS. E.: (*off*). Draw the curtains before you go, will you, dear? Thank goodness the days are drawing out again, though. I'm so sick of the winter.

JOSIE: O.K., Mum.

(*She moves to the french windows* L., *draws one of the curtains, and begins reading the letter.*)

(*Reading*). "My dear—You have just left, and I have found that you have left two pounds for me on the desk. How thoughtful of you, and, after that catechism of smug deficiencies you had just recited to me, how very practical and how like you. I suppose you must have slipped it there while I was swallowed up in the damned misery of our situation. Make no mistake—for the money, I'm grateful. But your setting up as a kind of emotional soup kitchen makes me spit.

(RUTH *is seen to fold her arms to her and shiver.*)

If you had any understanding at all, you would know what a bitter taste this kind of watery gruel must have. This is the Brown Windsor of love all right, and the only fit place for it is the sink. If this is the kind of thing you and your pals would dole out for the proletariat and its poor, grubby artists, you had better think again. I'm just going out for some beer. PS. Was just going to post this, when I thought I would return this watch to you. It seems to be the one thing I have left that you ever gave me. I'd like to think that my returning it would hurt you, but I know it won't."

(*Bell rings.*)

23

(*The lights in the sitting-room blaze on.* MRS. E. *has switched them on. The door bell goes on ringing furiously.*)

MRS. E.: My goodness, Josie, can't you please answer the front door for me? I've got milk on the stove. (*Into kitchen.*) And I asked you to draw those curtains, didn't I?

JOSIE: O.K. (*Draws curtains.*) All right, all right, I'm coming. (*Goes through hall to front door.*)
Oh, it's you. It's only Norah, Mum.
(NORAH *comes in, wearing outdoor clothes. She is in her middle thirties. She has some of her mother's restraint but this is due more to having "been let down twice". There is no bitterness, only a naïve simplicity in all things and at all times.*)

MRS. E.: That you, Norah?

JOSIE: (*going into sitting-room*). Well, I've just said so, haven't I?

NORAH: (*following her*). Can't think where I left my key. It's probably in my other bag. I'll have a look in a minute. (*Takes off hat and coat.*) Blessed train, packed as usual. (*Fetches her slippers from under the settee and changes her shoes.*) I saw Father coming up the road, but I wasn't going to wait for *him* to let me in. Not after this morning.
(JOSIE *takes out her "jazz" trousers and holds them against her waist, dancing and humming quietly.*)

MRS. E.: (*in kitchen*). Had a nice day, dear?

NORAH: Not bad, thanks, Mum. (*To* JOSIE.) You going to the club tonight?

JOSIE: I might. Why?

NORAH: Nothing.

JOSIE: Len's got a new motor-bike. It's a smasher.

NORAH: Fancy.

JOSIE: Mum says he can come to dinner on Sunday.

MRS. E.: (*in from kitchen*). Well, Mum has changed her mind. He can't.

JOSIE: Oh, Mum! Why?

MRS. E.: I'll tell you why later. For goodness' sake take that

24

blessed box upstairs. Supper's nearly ready and
there's only George and him to come.

(JOSIE *picks up box and trousers and goes upstairs, singing her favourite song.*)

NORAH: George who?

MRS. E.: Young George from the office, you know the one who gave me the necklace.

NORAH: Oh, him.

MRS. E.: Would you like to start your supper, dear? It's all ready, and I expect you're hungry. (*She goes into the kitchen.*)

NORAH: You know I'm never hungry, Mum.

MRS. E.: Too many sweets, my girl, that's your trouble. (NORAH *sits at her usual place at the table.*)

MRS. E.: You know what a state your teeth are in already. (*In with a plate of food which she places in front of* NORAH.) I'm sure those sweets are half the trouble. There, see how you like that.

NORAH: Thanks, Mum.

(MRS. E. *goes to the foot of stairs and calls.*)

MRS. E.: Ruth—Ruth, dear! Don't be long will you? And don't forget that towel. (*She returns to sitting-room.*) Is it all right dear?

NORAH: Yes, thanks.

MRS. E.: That's good.

(MRS. E. *goes into kitchen as the front door opens.* PERCY, *her husband, comes in with a brief-case, mac and umbrella, all of which he deposits at the hat-stand. He is a small, mean little man. Small in every sense of the word, with a small man's aggression. He goes upstairs.*)

NORAH: Mum!

MRS. E.: (*coming in*). Yes, dear? Something wrong?

NORAH: *He's* just come in, I think.

MRS. E.: Oh! (*Going to foot of stairs.*) Percy!—Was that you, Percy? (*She returns to sitting-room.*) I suppose it was him, Norah?

NORAH: Of course it was. I'd know that cat-like tread any-

25

where. Trust him not to give a civil answer to a civil question.

MRS. E.: The only time your father ever gave a civil answer to a civil question was when he said "I will" at the wedding.

Hope George isn't long, then we can all clear off into the lounge and watch the telly—leave your father to it. Anything on tonight? Not one of them morbid plays, I hope.

NORAH: There's some skating, I think.

MRS. E.: That'll be nice. (*Into kitchen.*) They usually have some nice music with that.

(PERCY *comes downstairs and, after taking an evening paper from his brief-case, goes into the sitting-room and sits at the table in the arm-dining-chair.*)

MRS. E.: (*lifting kitchen hatch*). Will you have boiled pork or boiled eggs?

PERCY: (*reading paper*). Nothing.

MRS. E.: You heard what I said—boiled pork or boiled eggs?

PERCY: And you heard what I said—nothing. Just a cup of tea.

(MRS. E. *slams down hatch.*)

(NORAH *pours out tea for her father and herself.*)

NORAH: Must put some more water in the pot.

PERCY: You'll drown it.

NORAH: And I know something else that needs drowning. (*Into kitchen with teapot.*)

(MRS. E. *comes in with plate of food, and sets it in front of* PERCY.)

PERCY: I said I didn't want anything.

MRS. E.: You'll no doubt eat it just the same. Josie! Ruth! Come along, now! And another thing: I hope you'll mind your manners, Percy, in future, particularly as I have a young gentleman from the office coming to stay here for a little while. (*To herself.*) It'll be like having Raymond in the house again.

PERCY: Accch! So you've taken to cradle-snatching, have you. Not content with taking another woman's

26

husband, ~~you have to~~ pick up a "young gentleman" ~~as well. Where did all this happen~~—Dean Street?

MRS. E.: (*with an effort*). Look, Percy, I'm warning you, once and for all, this is *my* house, and I have worked for every penny I bought it with, and everything in it. As far as I'm concerned, you're just the lodger here. Why you've got your knife into Jack Livings, goodness only knows. They're nice, respectable people, and well you know it. I'm sure I don't know what Mrs. Livings would say if she knew about your horrible accusations. Just because Mr. Livings comes in now and again to do a few useful things about the house, that's all it is—things you're too *damn* lazy to do for me.

NORAH: (*mildly*). Mum!

MRS. E.: I'm sorry, Norah, but there it is. There are times when your father goes too far with his insults. And I'll have you know this too: George is a fine, clean, upright young man. And he's clever too. He's in the theatrical line, he is, and one day he's going to be as famous as that Laurence Olivier, you see, and then perhaps you'll laugh on the other side of your face.

PERCY: Accch! Theatrical line! Don't give me that nonsense. I bet you he hasn't got two ha'pennies for a penny —they never have, these people.

MRS. E.: No—it's true that, at the moment, he hasn't a lot of money to throw around, but he will have, he's that type. He's used to money, you can tell that. He's very cultured.

NORAH: Not like some people we know.

PERCY: How is it he's only a tupenny-ha'penny penpusher then?

MRS. E.: He's not a clerk any longer. There was a little upset at the office today and he walked out. And a good job too, I say. Wasting his time and talent in a place like that. It's not right, and I wouldn't like to see any boy of mine going to waste like that—especially when George has so many plans and ideas to make

27

himself famous. There isn't much he can't turn his hand to in the theatrical line, believe me. Why he doesn't only act in plays, he writes them as well. As a matter of fact, he's bang in the middle of one at the moment. I expect he'll finish it while he's here.

PERCY: That's all very interesting, I'm sure. You've got it all nicely worked out between you, haven't you? But what about me? I'm going to look a proper bloody fool, aren't I? What are the neighbours going to think, I'd like to know?

MRS. E.: No more than they do now, believe me. They know very well what you're like. I haven't forgotten yesterday either—shouting and swearing at the top of your voice. At the front door too. The humiliation of it! I don't mind you swearing at the back door, but the front door—well——

PERCY: Accch! You women—nag, nag, nag.
(JOSIE *comes downstairs, and goes into the "lounge". She is now "respectable".*)

MRS. E.: Is that you, Ruth? Josie? Oh, for heaven's sake don't start looking at that thing till we've had supper.
(JOSIE *comes out of lounge into sitting-room.*)

JOSIE: Oh, all right. It's only the newsreel.
(*She gets a chair and sits at the table.*)
(MRS. E. *goes into the kitchen and returns immediately with two plates of food.*)
It's panel-game night, isn't it?

MRS. E.: There you are. (*She places plate in front of* JOSIE.) And I may as well have mine while I'm about it. And what do you say, Miss Josie? (*Sits at table.*)

JOSIE: Sorry. Thanks, Mum.

MRS. E.: That's better.
(*They are all eating now.*)
(*Pause.*)

JOSIE: Silence in the pig-market, let the old sow speak first.

MRS. E.: Pudding, Percy?

PERCY: No.

JOSIE: Trouble with you, Dad, is you talk too much.

PERCY: Accch!

JOSIE: Can I put a record on, liven things up a bit. Ever so sordid in here, like a mortuary.

PERCY: That blessed racket. If I had my way——

MRS. E.: It's Norah's wireless.

(JOSIE *puts on a record and returns to her seat.*)

JOSIE: The girls are taking a coach up to Salisbury on Sunday. You coming, Mum?

(RUTH *comes slowly down the stairs. Halfway down, there is a knock at the door.*)

MRS. E.: No, I don't think so, dear. I expect Norah will though. She's coach mad.

(RUTH *answers the front door and a man's voice is heard outside. It is* GEORGE DILLON.)

NORAH: That would be lovely.

GEORGE: I'm awfully sorry, but does Mrs. Elliot live here?

RUTH: Yes, she does. Did you want to speak to her?

GEORGE: Well, as a matter of fact she asked me to——

RUTH: Oh, I am sorry. Of course, you must be George. Do come in.

(GEORGE DILLON *enters. He is a little over thirty, boyish, yet still every year his age. He is short, not good-looking, but with an anti-romantic kind of charm. He displays at different times a mercurial, ironic passion, lethargy, offensiveness, blatant sincerity and a mentally picaresque dishonesty—sometimes almost all of these at the same time. A walking confliction in fact. Just at the moment he is rather shy, feeling his way. He is carrying a suitcase and a 'carry-all' bag.*)

GEORGE: Yes, that's right. Thank you.

RUTH: I'm Ruth Gray. Mrs. Elliot's sister.

GEORGE: How do you do?

(*They shake hands.*)

I seem to think we've met somewhere before, haven't we?

RUTH: Yes, I had that feeling too.

MRS. E.: There's someone in the hall. Is that you, Ruth? (*She rises and goes into the hall.*)

29

RUTH: Mr. Dillon has arrived, Kate.

MRS. E.: Oh, good. You found your way all right, then? Glad you remembered it was Targon Wood station you had to get out at—most people think Pelham Junction is nearer, but it isn't really. I didn't hear you ring the bell. I expect you're hungry, aren't you? Would you like a wash before supper? Bring your things up. (*Going upstairs.*) I'll show you where your room is and where you can find the toilet.
(GEORGE *follows her up.*)

GEORGE: That's very nice of you. I couldn't find the bell, so I knocked instead.

MRS. E.: Yes, I thought I didn't hear you ring.
(*They both disappear.* RUTH *stands looking up the stairs for a moment.*)

JOSIE: Must be nearly time for "Classics on Ice". I'm going to get a good seat before that fellow pinches it. (*Rising, she puts chair under table.*) Sounds ever so posh, doesn't he?

NORAH: I thought you were going to the club.

JOSIE: It's a woman's privilege to change her mind. (*Crosses into hall.*) Well, what's he like, Auntie? (RUTH *does not move.*) Auntie, what's he like?

RUTH: I don't know. Of course I don't. Why should I?

JOSIE: Oh, all right. I was only asking. Keep your hair on. (*Goes into lounge.*)
(RUTH *walks slowly into sitting-room and sits in arm-chair.* NORAH *collects dirty plates.* PERCY *is still reading.*)
(MRS. E. *comes downstairs into sitting-room.*)

MRS. E.: Well, that's that. Have you finished, Percy?
(PERCY *folds newspaper.*)

PERCY: Where's Henry Irving?

MRS. E.: Never you mind. I'd be grateful if you made yourself useful for once and made up the lounge fire.
(PERCY *rises and switches off radiogram and goes into lounge.* NORAH *takes things into the kitchen.*)
That's right, dear. Can't keep his hands off that

wireless, can he? Now, Ruth, what about your supper, dear?

RUTH: (*rising*). Oh, nothing for me, thanks. (*Crosses to small table.*) I think I'll just have some hot milk and go to bed. (*She picks up the small package containing the watch. The note is missing.*) Kate.

MRS. E.: Yes, dear? Why, Ruth, what is it? You look quite pale. If I were you——

RUTH: Has anyone been at this table at all? Have they, Kate?

MRS. E.: My dear, I'm sure I don't know. What a funny thing to ask. Why shouldn't they if they want to?

RUTH: There was a letter of mine here. Quite personal. A private letter. Someone has moved it.

MRS. E.: Now, Ruth, dear, don't go upsetting yourself over a little thing like that. I expect you'll come across it later on. You go upstairs and I'll bring you up some hot milk later on.

(MRS. E. *goes into the kitchen. Then* RUTH *goes into hall, halfway upstairs she stops for a moment, then comes down again, goes to lounge door, opens it and calls. There is the sound of the "Skater's Waltz" from within.*)

RUTH: Josie, come here a minute, will you?

JOSIE: Oh, what do you want, can't you see I'm watching the telly?

RUTH: Come here, please, when I ask you. (*She moves to the foot of the stairs as she waits.*)

JOSIE: (*at lounge door*). What do you want?

RUTH: Shut the door and come here.

(JOSIE *goes to her.*)

JOSIE: Well?

RUTH: Where is it?

JOSIE: Where's what? I don't know what you're talking about.

RUTH: You know damn well what. Give me that letter.

JOSIE: Oh, that. Oh, yes. (*Slowly, reluctantly, she withdraws letter from her jumper.*)

31

RUTH: Thank you very much. Kindly learn to keep your nose clean in future, will you?

JOSIE: So that's where you've been all these week-ends, with Jock. Does he wear a kilt?

RUTH: Mind your own damned business. (*Gives her a resounding smack across the face.*)
(JOSIE *yells. Enter* MRS. E.)

MRS. E.: Why, whatever's going on?

JOSIE: Going on! It's Auntie Ruth what's been going on. *Carrying* on more like—with a man—and paying him for it what's more.

RUTH: Just you dare read my letters again, and I'll do more than slap your face.

JOSIE: Don't you talk to me like that—you're not my mum.

MRS. E.: If what Ruth says is true, Josie, then I'm very ashamed. I thought I'd brought you up to behave like a lady. Never, never do that again, do you hear? Now kindly leave the room—but first say you're sorry to Auntie Ruth.

JOSIE: (*after some hesitation*). I'm sorry, Auntie Ruth. (*Goes off to lounge singing "If Jock could love me, love me. . . ."*)

RUTH: Slut! slut! slut!

MRS. E.: Ruth—that's no way to talk, and you know it. (RUTH *turns away*.)

MRS. E.: So things didn't work out then?

RUTH: No—I've just walked out on him, for better or for worse.

MRS. E.: But I don't understand. Josie said something about paying him——

RUTH: I don't have to buy my love—or do I? Yes, I gave him the odd pound or two, to keep him alive.

MRS. E.: But surely he could do a job of work?

RUTH: Job of work? He's a writer—the original starving artist in the attic—and I believed he had promise.

MRS. E.: Then why did you leave him?

RUTH: He's been a promising young man for too long. Youthful promise doesn't look too well with

32

receding hair. I've misjudged him—he's the complete flop, and I've spent nearly six years giving all I could to him, giving my love to him—such as it is.

MRS. E.: It's beyond me, dear. It's funny—you're the only one in the family who doesn't have patience or understanding. While you were enjoying yourself at college, we all had to go out to work. I can only say that college gave you a lot of funny ideas.

RUTH: That's right. Funny enough to make me do an inexcusable thing. When he told me he hadn't a penny, not even the price of a packet of cigarettes, I went to his jacket pocket, and inside I found a cheque for eight guineas for some book review or other he'd written. He hadn't even told me about it. Not only did he lie about the money, but he even kept his piffling little success from me. A brainless, cheap little lie. And that did it—the whole works collapsed, the whole flimsy works. (*She walks to the door.*) I suppose that's really why I left him. (*Exits upstairs.*)

MRS. E.: (*crossing to hallway*). George! Supper's ready dear. (*Returns to kitchen.*)
(GEORGE *comes down, looking over his shoulder. As* GEORGE *crosses hall,* NORAH *comes out of kitchen into hall. "Skater's Waltz" comes up good and loud.*)

NORAH: Hullo.

GEORGE: Hullo.

NORAH: Your supper's in there. I'm going to watch the skating. (*She goes into lounge.*)
(GEORGE *goes into sitting-room. He coughs slightly.*)

MRS. E.: That's right, dear, make yourself at home. Oh, that blessed telly, it's much too loud, isn't it? (*She crosses to lounge and opens door.*) Do put that telly down a bit, there's good children. We can't hear ourselves think in here. (*She goes back into sitting-room.*) There, that's better isn't it? You sit there, dear. (*He sits in* PERCY'S *place.*) They're all watching the telly, so you can have your supper in peace. And while we're alone, dear—I want you to treat this just as if

C 33

it were your home, just do whatever you like, won't you?

GEORGE: That's very kind of you, Mrs. Elliot. I just don't know what to say (*he puts out his hand*), I can only say that I won't impose myself on you for one minute longer than I can help. You're so very kind.

MRS. E.: I've never mentioned this before, but I'm helping you all I can because I feel that in some small way I'm helping my son, Raymond. He was killed in the war, you know. That's his picture over there.

GEORGE: Yes, I'm sorry.

MRS. E.: (*very simply*). He was a lovely boy. Clever, like you, artistic, too, but somehow he didn't seem to have that drive, that sort of initiative. Well, he didn't really have much chance to get on. But *you* will, George, I'm sure. With all your talent, you just can't go wrong. You're always planning things—and all the things you've already done too. You've got your acting and your plays and I don't know what, haven't you?

GEORGE: Oh, yes, Mrs. Elliot, don't you worry—the play I'm writing now is just about in the bag. I can finish it in no time here. And I've already got someone interested in it—for the West End, I mean.

MRS. E.: Well, there you are—what did I say? You certainly are one for irons in the fire, aren't you? And to think we shall all come and see your piece, and sit in the posh seats. That will be nice. Well, there we are, dear. And if Ray was here now, I'd be talking to him just as I'm talking to you. What I'm trying to say is that I want you to feel that you are taking his place in the home, and if there's anything you want—anything—please don't hesitate to ask. And don't, please, ever go short of money. Ray used to send me home so much a week when he was in the army, for me to save for him when he came home. I'd like to think it's being put to good use at last by helping you.

34

GEORGE: Bless you, Mrs. Elliot. (*He coughs slightly.*) You're so very kind and thoughtful. I just don't know how to thank you. I only hope I'll prove worthy of your kindness. I promise I won't let you down in any way. I promise you that.

MRS. E.: (*patting his cheek*). Good. Now we must see about getting you something to eat. Being a vegetarian you must eat lots of strange things. You'll have to tell me about them as we go along. (*Into kitchen.*)

GEORGE: I don't want you to put yourself out.
(*He sits looking around him.*)

MRS. E.: (*lifting hatch*). I've got some nice boiled cod and parsley sauce. You do eat fish, don't you? (*She sees him staring at the birds on the wall* c.) Yes, Ray painted those. I told you he was artistic, didn't I? (*Hatch down.*)
(GEORGE *rises and walks round the room restlessly, looking at the photographs on the wall, the cocktail cabinet, the general dressings. He then picks up the photograph of* RAYMOND *and looks at it steadily.*)

GEORGE: You stupid looking bastard.

(QUICK CURTAIN)

ACT II

Summer. There is now a telephone standing on small table in hall. The french windows are open. The settee brought round to face slightly downstage. NORAH, JOSIE, MRS. E., *and* PERCY *are sitting in their customary places at the meal table, eating. After curtain rises, a slight pause.*

MRS. E.: Pudding, Percy?

PERCY: No.

    (MRS. E. *rises, taking plates into kitchen. As she does so, the telephone rings and she stops dead.*)

NORAH: (*with awe*). It's ringing!

JOSIE: The phone's ringing!

MRS. E.: Our first call.

PERCY: What a racket—wireless, T.V., and now the blinking telephone.

MRS. E.: Who's it for, I wonder?

NORAH: Answer it and see.

JOSIE: Yes, that's the best way to find out. (*Jumps up and goes into hall.*) I'll go, Mum. (*Lifts receiver.*) Yes, yes it is. Who? Yes. All right, I'll fetch her. (*Into sitting-room.*) It's for you, Mum. Ever such a funny man—he's got a sort of Chinese accent.

MRS. E.: (*giving plates to* JOSIE). Chinese?

JOSIE: Yes.

MRS. E.: But I don't know any Chinamen.

JOSIE: Well, you'd better hurry up and answer it, Mum—he's waiting.

NORAH: Perhaps he's from *Chu Chin Chow on Ice.*

    (MRS. E. *goes into hall, and picks up receiver.*)

MRS. E.: Hullo. Yes, it is. (JOSIE *stands in doorway, listening.*) Have we what? Well, I don't know. I'll see. (*To* JOSIE.) He wants to know if we've got any laundry

36

that wants doing. (*In phone.*) No, I don't think so, thank you. What are you laughing at? (*She laughs.*) Oh, you are a naughty boy, you really are—you took us all in. (*To* JOSIE.) It's George.

JOSIE: Oh, silly. (*She goes into kitchen.*)

MRS. E.: What's that, dear? Have you? Oh, I am pleased. Yes, oh we will! All right, dear. Good-bye. (*Replaces receiver, goes into sitting-room.*) Says he's got some good news—he's got a job, and something about his play. I didn't quite catch what it was. Fancy young George being the first to ring up—and I had it put in specially for him too. Isn't that nice? Oh, I must sit down a minute—the excitement's too much for me! (NORAH *pours tea.*)

NORAH: Needs more water. (*Into kitchen.*)

PERCY: *What's* he gone and got?

MRS. E.: You heard, didn't you? A job. What did you think it was?

JOSIE: (*in from kitchen*). Must be something good for him to ring up like that.

MRS. E.: Yes—silly boy. He was only at the station. He'll be home in a minute. I'm so glad. That awful day he left that office, he swore he'd stick it out until he got something really worthwhile. (NORAH *comes in with teapot.*)

MRS. E.: And it's turned up at last. He always said he wouldn't take anything tatty.

NORAH: What's "tatty"?

MRS. E.: I don't really know, dear—George is always saying it.

JOSIE: Well, now I can really tell the whole of Targon Broadway that we've got a real actor staying with us. That's if he doesn't get too stuck up, and want to go and live in Berkeley Square or something.

MRS. E.: Of course he won't. George has settled down here very well. This is his home now. There's no reason at all why he should have to go.

JOSIE: Well, he'll have to get married sometime, won't he?

37

MRS. E.: Well, yes, there is that, of course.

NORAH: How do you know he hasn't got a girl friend already?
(*Phone rings.*)

MRS. E.: Well! There it is again—twice in a couple of minutes.
(JOSIE *goes to it quickly, lifts receiver.*)

JOSIE: (*on phone*). Hullo. Who? No, I think you must have
the wrong number. You're welcome. (*Puts phone
down and returns to sitting-room.*) Wrong number.

MRS. E.: Oh.

JOSIE: What were we talking about?

MRS. E.: George. I was just going to say that I think you're a
bit gone on him aren't you. What about poor old
Len Cook now, eh!

JOSIE: Well, George will do to fill in while Len does his
National Service. I wouldn't mind going to Germany
with Len though.

NORAH: You'd have to marry him first, wouldn't you? I
mean it wouldn't be very proper just to go and—
well—"live" with him——

JOSIE: Oh, I don't know. I don't mind what I do or where I
go, so long as my man's got money.

PERCY: The trouble with young girls today is that they
spend too much time thinking about love and
S-E-X.

JOSIE: S-E-X? Oh, sex. Sex doesn't mean a thing to me. To
my way of thinking, love is the most important and
beautiful thing in this world and that's got nothing
to do with sex.

PERCY: (*producing irrelevances like a bombshell*). Well, I may
be a crank and all that, but if I can persuade the
council to close the park gates after dark, I shall die
a happy man.

NORAH: What on earth's that got to do with sex?

MRS. E.: Well, I don't think we need go on with this
conversation—but Josie is quite right. You keep
those beautiful thoughts dear and you can be sure
you won't come to any harm. Put the kettle on for
George, there's a dear. (JOSIE *goes into kitchen.*)

38

(GEORGE *appears at the french window, waving a bottle of wine.*)

GEORGE: Friends, Romans and countrymen, lend me your ears!

MRS. E.: Oh, George! You did make me jump! (GEORGE *goes up and hugs her.*) And I'm so pleased about your job dear—we're all dying to hear about it.

JOSIE: Where is it, George, Drury Lane?

GEORGE: Could be, Josie, could be! Come on Norah, cheer up and find the corkscrew for the big Bacchanalia.

MRS. E.: I'll find it (*Goes to cocktail cabinet.*)

GEORGE: Cast of thousands, ten years in the making. Starring the one and only Mrs. Elliot as Juno!
(*They all laugh with the exception of* PERCY. RUTH *comes in at the front door and stands listening at the foot of the stairs.*)

GEORGE: (*assuming a thick Dublin accent*). And you, Norah, me darlin', you shall play Ariadne.

NORAH: I'm not being a man for you or nobody.

GEORGE: And Josie, let me see, yes, you'll play Semele.

JOSIE: Oh! There's a name to go to bed with!

GEORGE: And that's exactly what you do my sweet—with me, Jupiter.
(*More general laughter.*)
(RUTH *goes upstairs.*)

PERCY: Accch!

MRS. E.: There you are, Josie, what was I saying only a minute ago? (*Handing* GEORGE *corkscrew.*)

GEORGE: Now let the wine flow on this day of days. And what a day it's been. Do you know, one agent I went to see this morning looked me up and down in this duffel-coat and said: "No, we ain't got no *Biblical* parts today." Must have thought I looked like John the Baptist. Perhaps if I go in a kilt, he'll offer me a gangster part.
Glasses, Mrs. E. Bring out the golden goblets. That's right. For in spite of George continually being told he's too young, too old, too short—in

39

spite of his wig, glass eye, false teeth and wooden leg, George has got himself a job. (*He hands wine to* MRS. ELLIOT.) There we are.

MRS. E.: I mustn't have more than one. I can't go to the meeting tiddly, can I? I don't know what Mr. Colwyn-Stuart would say.

GEORGE: Josie?

JOSIE: I certainly won't say no. (*Takes glass.*)

GEORGE: And what about you, Percy. Will you have a tipple?

PERCY: Well, seeing as how you are in the money.

GEORGE: And Norah! A glass for Norah Mavourneen—me darlin' gal.

NORAH: Not for me, thank you.

GEORGE: No?

NORAH: No, thank you.

MRS. E.: Oh, go on, Norah. It's no use you pretending you're teetotal. You had some on Boxing Day, I remember. Go on, be sociable.

NORAH: I really don't think I could after seeing those great fat men on the telly last night trampling on the grapes half naked. It was horrible.

GEORGE: So Norah isn't going to touch any more wine until they bath in a respectable manner? Never mind, dear, just one sip won't hurt you. (*Gives her a glass.*)

NORAH: Oh, all right then, just a sip.

MRS. E.: Well, good health, George, and congratulations.

ALL: Good luck, Down the hatch, *etc.*

JOSIE: Well, now tell us what it is.

GEORGE: First of all, there's every chance of my play going on at the Trident Theatre.

MRS. E.: Oh, good.

JOSIE: Where's that, George? In the West End?

GEORGE: Well, no, not exactly. Bayswater. And it means I should get plenty of managers and agents to see it.

MRS. E.: Oh, good.

GEORGE: I saw Ronnie Harris this morning—you know the film man and he said he's got a part for me coming up shortly.

NORAH: What sort of film, George?

GEORGE: Don't really know yet—to do with some Army job or something, so he says.

MRS. E.: That'll be nice.

GEORGE: And finally, I've got a T.V. job coming up in three weeks' time.

JOSIE: George! You going to be on the telly?

GEORGE: Well, yes. But it's not exactly the lead, mind you, but it's something, anyway.

JOSIE: Oh, I'll say it is. Our George on the telly! What are you going to be in, George?

GEORGE: Ever heard of a play called *Hamlet*?

JOSIE: Of course I have.

NORAH: Yes, I saw that a long time ago. That's a very *old* one, isn't it. Very good though. He dies in the end, doesn't he?

GEORGE: He does indeed, Norah, he does.

NORAH: I always like a good laugh really. What I always say is——

NORAH: ⎱ There's enough misery in the world without paying
GEORGE: ⎰ to see it.

GEORGE: I don't think you really like the theatre very much, do you, Norah?

NORAH: Oh, yes I do.

GEORGE: Not really.

NORAH: Yes, but I don't ever go.

GEORGE: Oh, but you should. The theatre is like a shrine, Norah. A cathedral. Do you ever go to church, Norah?

MRS. E.: The only time she goes to church is when she's got a blessed banner stuck in her hand.

NORAH: Oh, Mum. (*Rises and goes into lounge.*)

MRS. E.: And talking of church—I must pop your Saviar in the oven. You'll be able to look after it, won't you? I'm off to the meeting as soon as Mr. Colwyn-Stuart gets here. (*Exit kitchen.*)

GEORGE: Lord, is he coming? I'm in no mood for Mr. Colwyn-pussy-Stuart. Josie, how long will you be?

JOSIE: How long will I be? Oooooh! It's jazz night! I must get changed. (*She runs upstairs.*)

GEORGE: (*sinking exhausted in arm-chair*). Tired as I am, anything would be better than having to put up with that moron.

PERCY: For once, young man, I agree with you. Thanks for the drink.

GEORGE: (*absently*). Not at all. A pleasure.

PERCY: Now that you're a celebrity, I'm surprised that you want to go jazzing at the Jubilee Hall with Josie.

GEORGE: (*singing*). "Jazzing at the Jubilee with Josie!"

PERCY: And I certainly hope that now you are earning money, you will be able to pay for yourself instead of sponging off other people.

GEORGE: (*looks at him sharply*). What do you mean?
(*The front doorbell rings.*)

MRS. E.: (*in from kitchen*). That's him now. Right on the dot as usual. Do I look all right?
(RUTH *comes downstairs.*)

GEORGE: Ravishing.

PERCY: Accch!

MRS. E.: (*into hall*). Answer that, Ruth dear, will you?
(*Into sitting-room.*) And if you can't make an effort to make yourself a little more pleasant, you'd better go and watch the telly.

PERCY: (*sitting down*). I'm busy.
(RUTH *opens front door.*)

MRS. E.: All right then. But I don't want any upsets tonight.
(GEOFFREY COLWYN-STUART *comes in and follows* RUTH *into sitting-room. He wears an elegant suit, with a beautifully laundered shirt, a carefully chosen green spotted tie, and breast pocket handkerchief to match. He is a pale, balding man in his late thirties, all sweetness and light.*)

MRS. E.: Oh come in Mr. Stuart, I'm nearly ready. You know everyone don't you?

GEOFFREY: Yes. Good evening everyone. Why, Mrs. Elliott, you look blooming tonight.

MRS. E.: Oh not really. I haven't had a minute since I came in.

GEOFFREY: But that's the secret, isn't it? Good evening Mr. Elliot. How are you?

PERCY: (*half rises, turning to greet* GEOFFREY *but finally doesn't*). How are you?

MRS. E.: You've met George, haven't you?

GEOFFREY: Oh, yes, we've met several times, haven't we?

MRS. E.: Yes. He's been here a long time now.

GEOFFREY: Like one of the family, in fact.

MRS. E.: Well, I won't keep you long. I'll just pop upstairs and put on a spot of powder, then I'm ready. George'll keep you entertained. He keeps *us* entertained, doesn't he?
(PERCY *makes a noise like an aborted whistle, which he keeps up for the next few minutes.* RUTH ~~sits~~ at the table, drinking tea*).

MRS. E.: Didn't you want to watch the television, Percy? George has had some good news today, haven't you, George? We've been ever so excited. He's going to be on the telly himself soon. You'll have to come round and see him when he is. I expect he'll tell you all about it. Make Mr. Colwyn-Stuart comfortable. Don't go without me, now! (*Into hall and upstairs*).

GEOFFREY: It's all right, you needn't hurry. We're early yet. (*Crossing left.*) What a dear she is.

GEORGE: Rather.

GEOFFREY: Mind if I sit here? (*At table.*)

RUTH: Do. There's some tea left, if you'd care for some.

GEOFFREY: No, thank you so much. I've just had dinner.

RUTH: Have you? We've just had supper. (*Removes wine to ~~cocktail cabinet.~~*) + glasses ~~~~ to kitchen.
(PERCY *taps the sides of his armchair pensively.*)

GEOFFREY: And how's the world treating you, Mr. Elliot? I suppose I should say "how are *you* treating the world?" After all, that's what really counts, isn't it?

PERCY: Not too badly, thank you.

GEOFFREY: Your wife's been telling me that you've not been

43

sleeping very well lately. I'm sorry to hear that.

PERCY: (*rubbing his nose*). Oh? She told you that, did she?

GEOFFREY: She mentioned it at our last meeting actually.

PERCY: The last meeting, was it? Actually?

GEOFFREY: How are you feeling now? Any better?

PERCY: Nothing the matter with me. Don't sleep so good sometimes, that's all.

GEOFFREY: Mrs. Elliot says she can't persuade you to go to a doctor about it.

PERCY: Don't believe in them.

GEOFFREY: Well, I think you'll find plenty of people to support you there—including you, eh, George?

GEORGE: Right.

PERCY: I don't believe in a lot of vegetarian rot either. I'm not making *my*self ill. Meatless steaks! (*Grins.*)

RUTH: Yes, I must say, that was rather too much for me. Nut cutlet I can take, but meatless steak's a bit too much of a paradox. Do you think Oscar Wilde could possibly have been a vegetarian?

PERCY: It's just that I have a lot of things on my mind.

GEOFFREY: In your own words, Mr. Elliot. Exactly. The old ravelled sleeve of care, am I right, George?

GEORGE: (*absently*). Eh?

RUTH: Shakespeare, George. Aren't you supposed to stand to attention, or something?

GEOFFREY: The number of people one sees every day, with tired, haggard eyes, dark circles of care underneath them.

GEORGE: I always thought that had another significance.

GEOFFREY: (*smiling*). You're a pretty free sort of chap, aren't you? I hope you don't shock everyone in this respectable household with your Bohemian ways.

GEORGE: By "Bohemian" I suppose you mean crummy. It's rather like calling bad breath "halitosis", don't you think?

RUTH: He's straight out of *Trilby*—didn't you know?

GEORGE: Frankly, I always touch mine up with a brown liner.

GEOFFREY: What?

GEORGE: The rings under my eyes—helps me when I play

44

clergymen's parts. I'm rather good at them.

GEOFFREY: (*refusing to be stung*). You know, you surprise me a little, George. You seem such an intelligent, vital young man, so much in the swim. After all, it's not even considered fashionable to be sceptical nowadays. The really *smart* thing is the spiritual thing.

RUTH: That's true enough.

GEOFFREY: And you too, Ruth. Of course, your interests are political, I know. But shall I tell you something? If I were to invite the Foreign Secretary, say, down here to speak, he wouldn't be able to half fill the Jubilee Hall.

RUTH: Are we supposed to be surprised?

GEOFFREY: On the other hand, if I were to invite someone like Billy Graham—well, take my word for it, you wouldn't be able to get within a mile of the place.

RUTH: With his message of love and all that? Love isn't everything, you know, Mr. Stuart.

GEOFFREY: That's where we disagree, Ruth. I believe that it is.

RUTH: Take justice away from love, and it doesn't mean a thing.

GEOFFREY: Love can change the face of the world.

RUTH: Tell that to the poor black devils in South Africa. Why don't you do something for them?

GEOFFREY: Dear, oh dear—we're going to get involved already if we're not careful. I can see that. Oh, there's nothing I enjoy more than a good old intellectual rough and tumble, and I only wish I could stay and slog it out with the two of you, but there isn't time, unfortunately. The fact is, we've probably got a great deal in common. You know: I have discovered a new way of judging people.

RUTH: You have?

GEOFFREY: I simply ask myself whether their lights are shining.

GEORGE: What about their livers?

GEOFFREY: (*laughing*). Yes. I did phrase it badly didn't I? Perhaps I should have said "lamps". I ask myself whether their lamps are shining. You see, my theory

45

is that inside every one of us is a lamp. When it's alight, the loves and hates, the ambitions, desires and ideas inside it are burning, and that person is really alive. But there are people who go around every day, at work, at home with their families—they seem normal, but their lamps have gone out. They've simply given up. They've given up being alive.

RUTH: And are our lamps alight, do you think, Mr. Stuart?

GEOFFREY: Oh, very definitely. It struck me the moment I came into the room.

GEORGE: Tell me. (*Nodding at* PERCY.) What about Mr. Elliot's lamp?

GEOFFREY: Oh, yes, I think so. I think so. It's burning all right.

GEORGE: You *think* so! You hear that, Percy? You need a new wick.

GEOFFREY: Oh, I hope I didn't sound rude. I think Mr. Elliot is on edge about things a little perhaps, principally because he's tired and can't sleep.

PERCY: All I said was——

GEOFFREY: People are wearing themselves out, worrying about a whole lot of things, unimportant things that don't matter one jot. You, Ruth, you worry about who's going to win the next election.

RUTH: Believe me—I no longer give a *damn*.

GEOFFREY: It's not important. And you, George, you worry about whether you're going to rise to the top of your profession. That's not important.

GEORGE: Thank you. We'll let you know.

GEOFFREY: One day—a few years ago this was—I happened to speak to a very famous clergyman—oh, he's dead now——

PERCY: He's all right then.

GEOFFREY: For years that man was in the habit of addressing as many as six different meetings in one day, often in the same number of towns. So I asked him how it was that he never seemed to get even a little bit tired. And he explained it to me. He said: "Because I believe in every single word that I utter."

46

GEORGE: Lucky him.

GEOFFREY: You could see his lamp burning at the very back of
the hall. He was on fire for what he believed in. And
that's the secret. It's no use sitting around moaning.
(*Enter* MRS. E. *from hall.*)

MRS. E.: Who's been moaning? I'm all ready. The television's
started, Percy. Have you been having a little chat
with George?

GEOFFREY: Well, not exactly. I'm afraid I've been rather bad
mannered.

MRS. E.: I'm quite sure you haven't. *You're* never bad
mannered with anyone.

GEOFFREY: I have been rather monopolizing the conversation. In
fact, I've a teeny weeny feeling that George and Ruth
think I'm rather an old bore.

MRS. E.: Of course he doesn't. He's a very deep one, George—
I know that.

GEOFFREY: What really started us off was—we were talking
about tiredness. It's a long time since I heard *you*
complaining of tiredness, Mrs. Elliot. ~~Not since those
very early days just after—just after the end of the
war.~~ I think she's a good advertisement for the
system, don't you? No doubt, it sounds a little odd
to you, but it's all a question of what *we* call
synchronizing yourself with Providence. Of getting
into step with the almighty.

MRS. E.: Yes. Well, I think we ought to be getting in step
ourselves, Mr. Stuart, don't you?

GEOFFREY: Yes, I suppose we had.
(*She turns to go, and* GEOFFREY *rises.* GEORGE *has
hardly been listening, but suddenly he responds, almost
as an afterthought to himself.*)

GEORGE: Yes. If only it were as simple as that, Mr. Stuart.
But life isn't simple, and, if you've any brains in your
head at all, it's frankly a pain in the arse.

MRS. E.: George! Really!

GEORGE: I'm sorry. I apologize. But I've said it now. You see,
to me there is something contemptible about a man

47

who can't face it all without drugging himself up to the rings round his eyes with a lot of comforting myths—like all these bird-brains who batten off the National Health. I don't care who it is—you or anyone—you must have a secret doubt somewhere. You know that the only reason you do believe in these things is because they *are* comforting.

GEOFFREY: So you think that religion is just a series of useful untruths?

GEORGE: Yes, I do.

PERCY: Hear! Hear!

MRS. E.: You be quiet!

GEOFFREY: It's all right, Mrs. Elliot. George is like so many young men—he believes that the great thing about the truth is that it must always be unpleasant.

GEORGE: It's just that I believe it's easy to answer the ultimate questions—it saves you bothering with the immediate ones.

MRS. E.: There's such a thing as faith, George.

GEORGE: I believe in evidence. And faith is believing in something for which there *is* no evidence. You don't say: I have faith that two and two are four, do you? Or that the earth is round? And why? Because they're both easily verified.

GEOFFREY: So it all has to be verified for you, does it, George? I think I understand you better than you know.

GEORGE: Oh?

GEOFFREY: You see, I come into contact with a great many artistic people. What *do* you believe in? Yourself?

GEORGE: Right. (*Adding in vocal parenthesis.*) He said, striking attitude of genius.

GEOFFREY: You have faith. You have faith in yourself—in your talent. Am I right?

GEORGE: Well?

GEOFFREY: Your talent, George. You believe in that with all your heart. And your evidence? Where is that, George? Can you show it to me?
(*Pause. They all look at him.*)

48

RUTH: *Touché.*

(GEORGE *is still for a moment. Then he laughs.*)

GEORGE: What a performance! All this Jesuit subtlety! You're too much for me. Just say that I'm like Christopher Columbus—I haven't discovered America yet. But it's there all right, waiting to be yes, verified.

GEOFFREY: Yes, I'm quite sure it is. You see, I have faith too. I can see the lamp burning. Well, we really must be off. Come along, Mrs. Elliot. Good night, everybody.

MRS. E.: Yes. Well, I shan't be back late.

(*They both go into hall, and out through the front door.*)

PERCY: (*rising and crossing to doorway*). Lamps! (*Chuckling.*) (*Turns.*) 'E ought to be on the bleeding stage—not you! (*Exit to lounge.*)

RUTH: Are you all right? You look a bit shaken.

GEORGE: I'm all right. I rather stupidly let the conducting of divine lip-service irritate me.

RUTH: So I noticed.

GEORGE: It's just been a pretty awful day, that's all.

RUTH: You surprise me.

GEORGE: Do I?

RUTH: Not really. You aren't very impressed with Geoffrey, I take it?

GEORGE: Right. What the Americans call "strictly for the birds". If there should be any heavenly purpose at all behind Mr. Colwyn-phoney-Stuart, it's that he's God's own gift to the birds. Hope I didn't upset Mrs. Elliot though. She's obviously pretty taken up with the whole racket.

RUTH: It might help if you weren't quite so vicious about it. You sound like a man with a secret doubt yourself.

GEORGE: Why is it you distrust me so much? I had a feeling we were the same kind.

RUTH: Did you? I suppose it's given poor Kate something to think about since Raymond was killed.

GEORGE: Tell me——

RUTH: Yes?

D   49

GEORGE: What was he really like?

RUTH: Raymond? Nice enough boy. Hard working, conscientious. Like most decent, ordinary lads of his age. (*Their eyes meet.*) You aren't remotely alike.

GEORGE: I thought you were in the habit of pitching into her yourself, hammer and sickle, over the Colwyn-Stuart.

RUTH: I should have thought that was different.

GEORGE: You mean that you're one of the family, and I'm not?

RUTH: If you like.

GEORGE: Suppose I'd better apologize.

RUTH: I shouldn't worry. I can't imagine what you could do wrong in her eyes. Well—I can imagine it all right, but I can't see you being stupid enough to lose the only good friend you've got.

GEORGE: What makes you think I haven't any good friends?

RUTH: Have you?

GEORGE: I thought you steel-hardened cadres of the far away left had a better defence against the little jokies of right wing deviationists like me. Or is it Wall Street jackal? No—I don't really look much like a jackal. Villiers Street wolf perhaps.

RUTH: Very droll—but not very well timed for someone who is supposed to be an actor.

GEORGE: Join my fan club, won't you?

RUTH: I'm not in the right frame of mind for shoddy little gags. (*Pause.*) I looked up the Party secretary tonight.

GEORGE: So you've packed it in at last.

RUTH: No doubt you think it's pretty funny.

GEORGE: No. I don't think it's funny.

RUTH: Seventeen years. It's rather like walking out on a lover. All over, finished, kaput. He hardly listened to my explanation—just sat there with a sneer all over his face. He didn't even have the manners to get up and show me out. I think that's what I've hated most of all, all these years—the sheer, damned bad manners of the lot of them.

GEORGE: Farther left you go, the worse the manners seem to get.

50

your to am chair shouted

RUTH: Well! The house is still fairly ringing with the bloody shovel of *your* opinions.

GEORGE: *I* have a sense of humour. "Bloody shovel of your opinions!" Is that a quotation? *turn to George*

RUTH: Just someone I used to know. Someone rather like you, in fact.

GEORGE: I thought you'd tied me up with someone the moment I met you.

RUTH: Where are you going tonight? *sit*

GEORGE: Dancing, I believe. Somewhere Josie knows.

RUTH: Don't sound so apologetic about it. It doesn't suit you. Pass my handbag, will you?
(*He does so.*)

RUTH: Looks as though you've a long wait ahead of you, my lad. (*She offers him a cigarette.*)

GEORGE: Have one of mine. (*Fumbles in his pockets.*)

RUTH: You needn't go through the pantomime for me, George. Take one.

GEORGE: No, thank you.

RUTH: Oh, don't look like that, for God's sake! You make me feel as though I'm—setting up as a soup kitchen or something. Please.
(*She throws a cigarette. He catches it, fumbles for a light. She snaps a lighter at him, and he goes over to her. He bends over her for a light.*)

GEORGE: How young you look sometimes.

RUTH: So do you when you're silent, and no longer trying to justify yourself. *light ——— cigarette.*

GEORGE: What's the time?

RUTH: Seven-fifteen. Where's your watch?

GEORGE: Being repaired.

RUTH: Pawned, I suppose.

GEORGE: Just as you like. I think I'll give Josie a yell.

RUTH: It won't do any good—not for ages yet. I didn't mean to hurt you just now.

GEORGE: Didn't you?

RUTH: Yes. You're quite right. I did mean to hurt you. I wish I hadn't.

51

GEORGE: What are you doing tonight?

RUTH: I don't know yet. I'm getting rather used to being at home every night. I *did* apologize.

GEORGE: We're neither of us as steel-hardened as we should be, are we? I used to smoke my mother's cigarettes too. Right up until the time she died.

RUTH: When was that?

GEORGE: Couple of years ago. We often used to go out together—she enjoyed that more than anything. She'd pay for the lot: drinks, meals, cinemas—even the bus fares. When the conductor came up the stairs, I would always grope in my pockets. And my mother would bring out her purse, and push my empty, fumbling hands away. "It's all right, dear. I've got change." I used to wonder whether perhaps there might come just *one* day when it might not have to happen. When I might actually have that two shillings or half-crown in my pocket. But it always did. It had become a liturgy. We went through it the last time we went out together—on my thirtieth birthday. During the war it was different. I was well paid then.

Even up to

RUTH: What did he give you for it?

GEORGE: What?

RUTH: The pawnbroker—for the watch?

GEORGE: Fifteen shillings. I was lucky to get that—it wasn't a very good one.

RUTH: Here. (*Takes out Jock's watch from handbag, and holds it out to him.*) Well, take it.

GEORGE: What's this?

RUTH: What does it look like? Try it on.

GEORGE: (*taking it*). Are you giving me this?

RUTH: Yes, but you don't have to make a meal out of it.

GEORGE: It must have cost a fortune.

RUTH: It did. Try not to pawn it. Or, if you do, tell me, and I can renew the ticket or something.

GEORGE: I shan't pawn it, I promise you. I think it must be the nicest present I've had. How do you fix it?

52

RUTH: Here—(*she adjusts it for him, he watches her*).

GEORGE: Your—friend?

RUTH: Oh, he doesn't want it any more. He told me.

GEORGE: Can you get the Third Programme on it?

RUTH: There!

GEORGE: Perhaps it'll change my luck.

RUTH: Superstitious too?

GEORGE: Thank you. Very much.
(*She still has his hand in hers.*)

RUTH: How beautiful your hands are—they're like marble, so white and clear.

GEORGE: Nonsense.

RUTH: But they are. I've never seen such beautiful hands.

GEORGE: You make it sound as if I were half dead already.
(*She looks up quickly, disturbed. Quite suddenly, he kisses her. Almost as quickly, he releases her. She soon recovers and moves away.*)

RUTH: Did you notice what I did with my lighter? My cigarette's gone out.

GEORGE: Didn't you put it back in your bag?
(*She opens it.*)

RUTH: So I did. What sort of parts do you play? On the stage, I mean.

GEORGE: Good ones.

RUTH: Stupid question deserves a stupid answer. I mean: any particular type.

GEORGE: I suppose so. Reminds me of the actor who was asked at an audition what sort of parts he played, and he replied "Scornful parts". I think I play "scornful" parts—anyone a bit loud-mouthed, around my height, preferably rough and dirty, with a furnace roaring in his belly. The rougher and dirtier the better.

RUTH: A character actor in fact.

GEORGE: I'm sorry I kissed you. So you needn't try to pay me back for it.

RUTH: Don't apologize. I was flattered for a moment. I'm sure there's an explanation somewhere, but I'd rather

53

you didn't try to tell me what it is.

GEORGE: Just as you like.

RUTH: First time I've tasted Brown Windsor.

GEORGE: Tasted what?

RUTH: (*laughing*). The Brown Windsor of love, George. Haven't you come across it.

GEORGE: That—friend of yours sounds rather pretentious to me.

RUTH: It's funny how rhetorical gentle spirits can become.

GEORGE: He's a poet or something?

RUTH: I used to hope so.

(GEORGE *stretches himself*.)

GEORGE: God, I feel tired!

(*He looks all round the room. His eyes rest on Raymond's painted birds on the back wall* C.) Blimey! Those birds! (*Goes upstage and walks around and is finally stopped by the sight of the cocktail cabinet*.) I've sat here for weeks now and looked at that. Oh, I've often marvelled at them from afar in a shop window. But I never thought I'd ever see one in someone's house. I thought they just stood there, in a pool of neon, like some sort of monstrous symbol, surrounded by bilious dining-room suites and mattresses and things. It never occurred to me that anyone bought them!

RUTH: Norah's cocktail cabinet? Well, she didn't actually buy it—she won it.

GEORGE: What was her reaction?

RUTH: I think we were all a little over-awed by it.

(GEORGE *goes nearer to it*.)

GEORGE: It looks as though it has come out of a jelly-mould like an American car. What do you suppose you *do* with it? You don't keep drinks in it—that's just a front, concealing its true mystery. What do you keep in it—old razor blades? I know, I've got it!

(*He sits down and "plays" it vigorously, like a cinema organ, humming a "lullaby-lane" style signature tune. He turns a beaming face to* RUTH.)

54

And now I'm going to finish up with a short
selection of popular symphonies, entitled "Ever-
greens from the Greats", ending up with Beethoven's
Ninth! And don't forget—if you're enjoying yourself,
then all join in. If you can't remember the words, let
alone understand 'em, well, just whistle the tune.
Here we go then!
(*Encouraged by* RUTH'S *laughter*, *he turns back and
crashes away on the cocktail cabinet*, *pulling out the
stops and singing:*
      "I fell in love with ye- ieuw!
       While we were dancing
       The Beethoven Waltz! . . ."
(*A final flourish on the invisible keyboard; he turns and
bows obsequiously.* RUTH'S *response has exhilarated
him, and he stands in front of her, rather flushed.*)
It ought to disappear somehow, but I couldn't find
the combination. (*He watches her with pleasure.*)
That's the first time you've ever laughed.

RUTH: Oh, yes, you can be funny, George. These flashes of
frenzy, the torrents of ideas they can be quite funny,
even exciting at times. If I don't laugh, it's because
I know I shall see fatigue and fear in your eyes
sooner or later.

GEORGE: Oh?

RUTH: You're burning yourself out. And for what?

GEORGE: Go on—but don't think you can kill my confidence.
I've had experts doing it for years.

RUTH: I just can't make up mind about you.

GEORGE: Meaning?

RUTH: Do you really have any integrity?

GEORGE: What's *your* verdict?

RUTH: I'm still not sure. It just seems to me that for someone
who makes a religion out of being brilliant, you must
be very unlucky.

GEORGE: You don't even begin to understand—you're no
different from the rest. Burning myself out! You bet
I'm burning myself out! I've been doing it for so

many years now—and who in hell cares? At this
moment I feel about as empty and as threadbare as
my pockets. You wonder that I should be tired. I
feel played out.

(*She applauds.*)

RUTH: Bravo! Not bad at all, George. Bit ragged maybe,
but it'll do. Perhaps you may not be so bad after
all. Tell me about this television job.

GEORGE: That? It's a walk-on—one line which will be drowned
by the rest anyway. And if I know Lime Grove, it'll
be so dark, I shan't be seen at all. All for twelve
guineas. It's a fortune. But what am I going to do?
How can I let them all sit in there—and probably
half the street as well—staring stupidly at the telly
for two and a half hours to watch me make one
thirty-second appearance at the very end? What a
triumph for dear old Percy! And Mr. Colwyn-Stuart
and his Hallelujah Chorus!

RUTH: Quite a problem.

GEORGE: As it is, I owe Mrs. Elliot God-knows how much.
But I suppose you knew that.

RUTH: It's not exactly a surprise.

GEORGE: She was buying me cigarettes every day up until last
week. I did manage to put a stop to that. I told her
I was giving it up for my health. To my surprise, she
actually believed me.

RUTH: *Are* you any good, George?

GEORGE: (*almost like a child*). That's a moron's question.

RUTH: As you like.

GEORGE: Well, ask yourself. Isn't it? Listen: all I ever got—
inside and outside the theatre—is the raves of a
microscopic minority, and the open hostility of the
rest. I attract hostility. I seem to be on heat for it.
Whenever I step out on to those boards—immediately,
from the very first moment I show my face—I know
I've got to fight almost every one of those people in
the auditorium. Right from the stalls to the gallery,
to the Vestal Virgins in the boxes! My God, it's a

56

gladiatorial combat! Me against Them! Me and
mighty Them! Oh, I may win some of them over.
Sometimes it's a half maybe, sometimes a third,
sometimes it's not even a quarter. But I *do* beat them
down. I beat them down! And even in the hatred of
the majority, there's a kind of triumph because I
know that, although they'd never admit it, they
secretly respect me.

RUTH: What about this film you're going to be in?

GEORGE: It doesn't mean a thing. The old line. You know?
Keep in touch—we'll let you know. You *don't*
understand do you?

RUTH: I just don't see much virtue in trying to ignore
failure.

GEORGE: There's no such thing as failure—just waiting for
success.

RUTH: George—really!

GEORGE: All right, forget it.

RUTH: I know what it is to go on waiting.

GEORGE: And do you think I don't! I spend my life next to a
telephone. Every time it rings is like death to me.

RUTH: (*relentless*). What about these plays you write. You
do do that as well, don't you?

GEORGE: Oh yes—you think I'm a dabbler. A dilettante who
can't afford it.

RUTH: This Trident Theatre—the "three uplifted fingers of
Drama, Ballet and Poetry——"

GEORGE: A so-called club theatre, meaning a preciously over-
decorated flea-pit, principally famous for its rather
tarty bar, and frequented almost exclusively by
intense students, incompetent longhairs, and rather
flashy deadbeats generally.

RUTH: I see. I'd like to read some of your work.

GEORGE: Thank you, I'll think about it.

RUTH: Do you charge a fee?

GEORGE: You're not being very funny yourself now.

RUTH: Perhaps your sense of humour has deserted you after
all. My politics and your art—they seem to be like

57

Kate's religion, better not discussed. Rationally, at any rate.

GEORGE: I knew you were suspicious of me, that you distrusted me. I didn't realize you detested me this much.

RUTH: George, why don't you go?

GEORGE: Go?

RUTH: Leave this house. Get out of here. If you're what you believe yourself to be, you've no place in a house like this. It's unfair to you. It's stifling. You should be with your own kind. And if you're not what you say you are, you've no right to be here anyway, and you're being unfair to everyone.

GEORGE: Are you serious? I haven't got a penny in the world.

RUTH: You'll manage. You've got to. It's your only chance of survival. Am I being harsh, George? Perhaps, as you say, we're the same kind.

GEORGE: (*savagely*). That's good! Oh yes! And what about you?

RUTH: (*off her balance*). What about me?

GEORGE: What are *you* doing here? All right, you've had your go at me. But what about yourself?

RUTH: Well?

GEORGE: Oh, don't be so innocent, Ruth. This house! This room! This hideous, God-awful room!

RUTH: Aren't you being just a little insulting?

GEORGE: I'm simply telling you what you very well know. They may be your relations, but have you honestly got one tiny thing in common with any of them? These people——

RUTH: Oh, no! Not "these people"! Please—not that! After all, they don't still keep coals in the bath.

GEORGE: I didn't notice. Have you looked at them? Have you listened to them? They don't merely act and talk like caricatures, they *are* caricatures! That's what's so terrifying. Put any one of them on a stage, and no one would take them seriously for one minute! They think in clichés, they talk in them, they even feel in them—and, brother, that's an achievement! Their

58

existence is one great cliché that they carry about
with them like a snail in his little house—and they
live in it and die in it!

RUTH: Even if it's true—and I don't say it is—you still
sound pretty cheap saying it.

GEORGE: Look at that wedding group. (*Points to it.*) Look at
it! It's like a million other grisly groups—all tinted
in unbelievable pastels; round-shouldered girls with
crinkled-up hair, open mouths, and bad teeth. The
bridegroom looks as gormless as he's feeling lecherous,
and the bride—the bride's looking as though she's just
been thrown out of an orgy at a Druids' reunion!
Mr. and Mrs. Elliot at their wedding. It stands there
like a comic monument to the macabre farce that
has gone on between them in this house ever since
that greatest day in a girl's life thirty-five years ago.

RUTH: Oh, a good delivery, George. You're being brilliant,
after all. They're very easy people to score off, but,
never mind, go on!

GEORGE: There's Josie—at this moment putting all she's got
into misapplying half Woolworths on to her empty,
characterless little face. Oh, sneer at me for my
snobbery, for my bad taste, but, say what you like:
I have a mind and feelings that are all fingertips.
Josie's mind. She can hardly spell it. And her feelings
—what about them? All thumbs, thumbs that are fat
and squashy—like bananas, in fact, and rather sickly.

RUTH: You should look an intriguing couple on the dance
floor tonight. I'm tempted to come myself.

GEORGE: Why don't you?

RUTH: I should hate to break up this marriage of true
minds.

GEORGE: You know damned well why I'm going. People like
me depend upon the Josies of this world. The great,
gaping mass that you're so fond of. You know? And
for tonight, Josie is that mass, all rolled into one.
And do you know what? Behind that brooding cloud
of mascara, she's got her eye on George, Josie

59

has. Because not only does she suffer from
constipation, but night starvation as well. And then,
there's Norah. Now what can you say about her?
Norah doesn't even exist—she's just a hole in the air!

RUTH: You've a lot to learn yet, George. If there weren't
people like the Elliots, people like you couldn't exist.
Don't forget that. Don't think it's the other way
around, because it's not. They can do without you,
take my word for it. But without them, you're lost—
nothing.

GEORGE: Don't give me that, Ruth. They drive you mad, and
you know it. It's like living in one of those really bad
suitable-for-all-the-family comedies they do all the
year round in weekly rep. in Wigan. How have you
stuck it here? What's the secret? Tell me. Since that
mysterious divorce of yours that they all heavy-
handedly avoid mentioning—and the week-end trips
you don't make any more. How long is it you've been
here? How long? Nine years is it? Ten years? Twelve?
Oh no, Ruth—*you* can't afford to sneer at me!

RUTH: You've made your point. Don't get carried away
with it. Why do I stay? Because I don't earn enough
to get me out of it, and somewhere else. I spend too
much on clothes, cigarettes——

GEORGE: And—"incidentals"? (*Holding up wrist-watch.*)

RUTH: The job I do is so hysterically dull that every time I
go into that office, and see myself surrounded by
those imitation human beings, I feel so trapped and
helpless, that I could yell my lungs out with the
loneliness and the boredom of it.

GEORGE: So you do!

RUTH: But, at my age, and with my lack of the right kind of
qualifications, there's not much else I can do. Perhaps
I haven't the courage to try. At least, I'm safe. And
so I go on, from spring, through the summer, to the
autumn and another winter, meaningless; just another
caricature.

GEORGE: I knew it! I knew it!

60

RUTH: Thank you for reminding me of it.

GEORGE: The truth is a caricature.

RUTH: Is that meant to be profound?

GEORGE: You hate them, don't you? Shall I tell you why they horrify me?

RUTH: I suppose I give you what is known as the "feed" line now. No—tell me, why do they horrify you.

GEORGE: They've no curiosity. There are no questions for them, and, consequently, no answers. They've no apprehension, no humility——

RUTH: Humility! (*Laughing.*) Good old George!

GEORGE: And, above all, no real laughter. Tell me, have you ever heard any of them, even once, laugh? I mean really laugh—not make that choked, edgy sound that people make all the time. Or, to put it more unintelligibly: I don't mean that breaking wind people make somewhere between their eyebrows and their navels, when they hear about the old lady's most embarrassing moment. I mean the real thing— the sound of the very wit of being alive. Laughter's the nearest we ever get, or should get, to sainthood. It's the state of grace that saves most of us from contempt.

RUTH: Hooray!

GEORGE: No, it wasn't really spontaneous. Singing and dancing "Jazzing at the Jubilee with Josie".

RUTH: Why haven't we talked like this before. A few moments ago you made me feel old. Now, I suddenly feel younger.

GEORGE: "If you can't give a dollar, give me a lousy dime . . ."

RUTH: Can't say I've exactly heard *you* falling about with mirth since you came here.

GEORGE: No, you haven't. I suppose it does sound as though I'm complaining because everyone doesn't go around as if they were on parole from "Crime and Punishment", muttering about God, and laughing their blooming heads off.

RUTH: Oh yes, you are a character! I think your little

61

performance has done me good.

GEORGE: You're a good audience. Even if I do have to beat you down. That's all I need—an audience.

RUTH: And do you—think you'll find it?

GEORGE: I don't know.
(*He takes a deep breath, and sits down quickly, suddenly drained. She watches him, fascinated.*)

RUTH: How quickly you change! That's what's so frightening about you. These agonizing bubbles of personality, then phut! Nothing. Simply tiredness and pain.

GEORGE: I've been trailing around all day. I've had a few drinks, and nothing to eat. It suddenly hit me, that's all.

RUTH: Perhaps you have got talent, George. I don't know. Who can tell? Even the experts can't always recognize it when they see it. You may even be great. But don't make a disease out of it. You're sick with it.

GEORGE: It's a disease some of us long to have.

RUTH: I know that. I met it once before.

GEORGE: Then you must know it's incurable.

RUTH: Galloping—like a consumption.

GEORGE: (*sharply*). What did that mean?

RUTH: Nothing.

GEORGE: But do you know what is worse? Far, far worse?

RUTH: No, Brother Bones, tell me what is worse.

GEORGE: What is worse is having the same symptoms as talent, the pain, the ugly swellings, the lot—but never knowing whether or not the diagnosis is correct. Do you think there may be some kind of euthanasia for that? Could you kill it by burying yourself here—for good?

RUTH: Why do you ask me?

GEORGE: Would the warm, generous, honest-to-goodness animal lying at your side every night, with its honest-to-goodness love—would it make you forget?

RUTH: All you're saying is that it's a hard world to live in

62

if you're a poet—particularly if it should happen that you're not a very good poet.

GEORGE: Unquote.

RUTH: Unquote. Life is hard, George. Anyone who thinks it isn't is either very young or a fool. And you're not either. Perhaps even bad artists have their place in the scheme of things.

GEORGE: Scheme of flaming things! Get us with our intellectual sets on! And we're not even tight. I wish we were spending the evening together, all the same.

RUTH: Why are you so morbidly self-conscious? I thought all actors revelled in exhibitionism.

GEORGE: Don't you believe it. Only insincere old bastards who carried spears with Martin Harvey, and have been choking themselves silly with emotion ever since. "Emotion, laddie—that's the secret!" Shall I tell you a story. Yes, do tell me a story. Well, it happened to me when I was in the R.A.F. during the war.

RUTH: I didn't know you were. You've never mentioned it.

GEORGE: The one thing I never shoot lines about is the R.A.F. Just a gap in my life. That's all. Well, it happened like this: It was one night in particular, when it wasn't my turn to go on ops. Instead, we got a basinful of what we gave the Jerries, smack bang in the middle of the camp. I remember flinging myself down, not so much on to the earth as into it. A wing commander type pitched himself next to me, and, together, we shared his tin-helmet. Fear ran through the whole of my body, the strange fear that my right leg would be blown off, and how terrible it would be. Suddenly, the winco shouted at me above the din: "What's your profession?"

"Actor," I said. The moment I uttered that word, machine-gun fire and bombs all around us, the name of my calling, my whole reason for existence—it sounded so hideously trivial and unimportant, so divorced from living, and the real world, that my fear vanished. All I could feel was shame.

63

(*He is lost for a moment or two. Then he looks at her quickly, and adds brightly.*)
Gifted people are always dramatizing themselves. It provides its own experience, I suppose.

RUTH: How pompous can you get? You had me under your spell for a moment. Now you've broken it. I'm beginning not to know when you're being real, and when you're not.

GEORGE: Always put the gun in the other man's hand. It's my rule of life.

RUTH: Yes. You're play acting all right. You've done it all your life, and you'll go on doing it. You can't tell what's real and what isn't any more, can you, George? I can't sit here drivelling all night.
(*She turns to go.*)

GEORGE: (*taking her by the arm*). And what if I do? What does it matter? My motives aren't as simple as you like to think——

RUTH: —You're being phoney, George, aren't you? We're a pair of——

GEORGE: —What if I am? Or you, for that matter? It's just as——

RUTH: (*sings*). "It's a Barnum and Bailey world,
　　　　Just as phoney as it can be!"
You've got us both acting it now——

GEORGE: —just as serious and as complex as any other attitude. Ruth! Believe me, it isn't any less——

RUTH: —haven't you, George? Cutting in on each other's lives——

GEORGE: —real or sincere. You just never stop standing outside——

RUTH: —fluffing your emotions——

GEORGE: —it's a penance——

RUTH: —that's the word, isn't it? You're fluffing it——

GEORGE: —the actor's second sense——

RUTH: —all studied, premeditated——

GEORGE: —watching, observing, watching me now, commenting, analysing, giggling——

64

RUTH: —timed for effect, deliberate, suspect——

GEORGE: —just at this moment, don't you want me more than anything else——

RUTH: ⎫ I've had my lot, George.

GEORGE: ⎮ More than anything?

RUTH: ⎮ We've both had our lots!

GEORGE: ⎬ You're as arrogant as I am!

RUTH: ⎮ You know what, George?

GEORGE: ⎭ That's one of the reasons you're drawn to me! If only you knew—how much—at this moment——

RUTH: No, not me. Somebody else—not me!

GEORGE: I mean it, damn you!

RUTH: Strictly for the birds, George! Strictly for the birds!

GEORGE: Ruth!

RUTH: Let me go!

(*He does so.*)

GEORGE: (*simply*). I've botched it. (*Pause.*) Haven't I?
The descent has been so sudden, and they are both dazed.

RUTH: I'm not sure what has happened. Nothing I suppose. We're just two rather lost people—nothing extraordinary. Anyway, I'm past the stage for casual affairs. (*Turns away.*) You can't go on being Bohemian at forty.

(JOSIE *comes running down the stairs into the sitting-room. She is wearing her "jazz trousers".*)

JOSIE: Ready?

GEORGE: Yes. Yes, I suppose so.

(RUTH *goes quickly out through the french windows.*)

JOSIE: Well, come on then. Had your supper?

GEORGE: No. I don't want anything. Let's have a drink, shall we, before we go?

JOSIE: Oh yes, lovely!

(GEORGE *does not move.*)

Well, what are you standing there for? What are you thinking about.

GEORGE: What am I thinking about? (*To cocktail cabinet for the wine.*) What am I thinking about? (*Pouring *drinks*.) Do you realize, Josie, that that is a lover's question? "What are you thinking about?" (*Hands her a drink*.)

JOSIE: Oh, you are daft. You make me laugh when you talk in riddles. Oh, well, cheers!

GEORGE: Cheers. It'll be tonight, Josephine. (*Drinks*.)

JOSIE: Whatever are you talking about? You are in a funny mood, I must say. Let's have some music while we finish our drinks. (*She goes to radiogram*.) We don't want to get there too early, do we?

GEORGE. All the best people arrive late.

JOSIE: (*looking through records*). What shall we have? There's "Mambo Man", "Jambo Mambo", or "Marmalade Mambo".

GEORGE: Oh, let's have something to soothe my rather shabby soul, Josie.

JOSIE: Go on, you haven't got one. What about this then? (*She puts on Mantovani*.)

GEORGE: (*screwing up his face*). Heaven. (*They begin dancing*.) Sheer heaven.
(*After a moment*.)

JOSIE: Bit boring isn't it—the music I mean.

GEORGE: The preliminaries always are, Josie, my girl. But they make anticipation all the more exciting. Are you ever excited by anticipation?

JOSIE: No, not really. Only when I see fellows like Len Cook, he's lovely.

GEORGE: That's not anticipation, Josie, that's lust, plain lust. Although it never is really plain. Do you know what lust is, Josie?

JOSIE: Of course I do, silly.

GEORGE: Lust, the harshest detergent of them all, the expense of spirit in a waste of shame. Or as Jean Paul Sartre put it—sex.

JOSIE: We were only talking about sex a little while ago. Boring, I think.

GEORGE: Do you? Shall we go?

JOSIE: All right.

(They move into the hall. At the foot of the stairs,
GEORGE *stops her.)*

GEORGE: Have you ever been kissed, Josie?

JOSIE: Hundreds of times.

GEORGE: Like this?

*(He kisses her fiercely. The lounge door opens and they
do not see* PERCY *standing there.)*

*(*RUTH *comes in through french windows, switches out
main lights, leaving just a glow in the sitting-room.*
PERCY *remains silhouetted against the light from the
lounge as* RUTH *sits in arm-chair.)*

JOSIE: George—don't George, there's somebody coming!

GEORGE: I've never tried the etchings line—*(leading her up the
stairs)*—let's see if it really works.

JOSIE: But George——

GEORGE: Come and see my etchings. *(They are by now halfway
up stairs.)*

JOSIE: What are you——

*(*GEORGE *smothers her with another kiss.)*

GEORGE: Silly girl.

JOSIE: But, George, what will Mum say?

(They are swallowed up in darkness. PERCY *moves
towards the foot of the stairs and looks up. Then he
moves into the sitting-room and looks down at* RUTH
for a moment. She is suddenly aware of him.)

RUTH: Why, Percy, how long have you been there?

PERCY: Long enough, I think. Quite long enough.

QUICK CURTAIN

ACT III

Scene One

Autumn. One french window is open. GEORGE *is lying on the settee in his shirt sleeves. His jacket is hung on the back of one of the chairs. There are some loose leaves of manuscript scattered by the side of the settee. After a moment,* GEORGE *shivers, gets up, and puts on his jacket.* MRS. E. *comes downstairs into the sitting-room with a breakfast tray.*

MRS. E.: Are you feeling any better, dear. You need not have got up at all, you know. (*She puts tray on table.*) Silly boy—the window open too. (*Crossing to window.*) You'll catch your death. The chrysanths have gone off. Chrysanths always remind me of Father. (*Stands at the window.*) (*Shuts window.*) Oh, dear, the clocks go back tonight. Awful, isn't it. (*Picks up tray.*) You didn't eat much breakfast, dear. (*Into kitchen.*) Your bed's made and your room is done if you want to go up any time. Nearly twelve—(*in from the kitchen*) the others will be back soon. Sure you're all right, dear? Everyone's a bit down in the dumps these days. It must be the winter coming on. Not that I mind it really. It's the awful in-between that gets me down. How's the writing going? All right?

GEORGE: Oh, not too bad, Mrs. Elliot, thanks. Feeling a bit whacked at the moment though.

MRS. E.: Well, you mustn't overdo it, you know. I'll get in some nice cakes for your tea.

GEORGE: Please don't do that, Mrs. Elliot dear, you know I don't eat them.

MRS. E.: All right, dear, just as you like. (*Going to him.*) I'm ever so sorry about the money, dear. Something will

68

turn up soon I expect—don't worry, dear. Raymond's money didn't go as far as we thought it might, did it? Still, never mind. As long as I've got a shilling or two, I'll see that you're all right. Now I really must go and get some shopping done. I hate Saturdays— the crowds are awful. (*Crosses into hall, and puts on coat.*)

(*The doorbell rings.*)

Oh, that'll be the milkman. Now where's my bag? (*She picks it up from the hallstand, and goes to the front door.*) Oh yes, yes, he does. Won't you come in? (MRS. E. *stands back to admit a tall, official looking man. He carries a brief-case.*)

MAN: Thank you.

(*They go through the hall towards the sitting-room.*)

MRS. E.: I'd better show you the way. He's not feeling so good today. Still, it'll be a nice break for him, having someone to chat to. (*In sitting-room.*) George, dear, someone to see you. Well, I'll leave you to it, if you don't mind. (*Exit through front door.*)

MAN: You are Mr. George Dillon?

GEORGE: That's right.

MAN: I'm from the National Assistance Board.

GEORGE: Oh yes, I wondered when you were coming. Please sit down.

MAN: Thank you.

(*He does so. Then opens brief-case, and extracts papers, file, etc., and fountain pen from jacket. He studies papers for a moment.*)

Hmm. Now, with regard to your claim for assistance —you are Mr. George Dillon?

GEORGE: I thought we'd cleared that up just now.

MAN: (*making notes*). And you are residing at this address, paying rent of thirty shillings a week?

GEORGE: Right.

MAN: What does that entail the use of? A bedroom, and general run of the house, I take it?

GEORGE: Yes.

MAN: May I trouble you for your rent book?

GEORGE: Well, as a matter of fact, I haven't got one. Not right now, that is. I could get you one, if it's really necessary.

MAN: You understand we have to examine your rent book, Mr. Dillon, in order to ascertain the correctness of your statement regarding the thirty shillings which you claim is being paid out by you in the way of rent each week.

GEORGE: Yes, of course.

MAN: So would you please make sure you are in possession of one, the next time I call.

GEORGE: Does that mean that I'll have to wait until then before I get any money?

(PERCY *comes in at the front door.*)

MAN: I'm afraid I can't answer that at the moment, Mr. Dillon. Now, let me see. You are, by profession, an actor?

GEORGE: Yes, I am—by profession.

MAN: Have you any idea when you are likely to be working again?

GEORGE: It's rather difficult to say.

MAN: In the near future, would it be?

GEORGE: That phone might ring at this moment with something for me. Or it may not ring for months. It might not even ring at all.

MAN: You seem to have chosen a very precarious profession, Mr. Dillon.

GEORGE: This money means rather a lot at the moment. I need—something—to show, you see——

MAN: Isn't there something else you could do, in the meantime perhaps?

GEORGE: Do you think I haven't tried? Incidentally, I am rather anxious that no one in the house should know about this——

MAN: Yes, of course.

(PERCY *enters sitting-room, and sits down.*)

MAN: Yes. I see. Well, Mr. Dillon, I can only hand in my

70

report as I see things, and see what happens. The board is very hesitant about—paying out money to strong, healthy men.

GEORGE: Of course. Is there anything else? (*Looking at* PERCY. *The Assistance Man is not quite sure what to do*.)

MAN: There's just the little matter of your last job. When was that?

GEORGE: Oh, about three months ago—television.

PERCY: Accch! You don't call that a job, do you? You could hardly see it was him. *We* knew it was him all right —but you had to be sharp to catch him.

MAN: Well, that'll be all I think, Mr. Dillon. (*Rising*.) You won't forget your rent book, will you?

PERCY: Rent book. Rent book! He hasn't got one! Shouldn't think he's ever paid any!

GEORGE: He knows that, you idiot. Well, I'll show you to the door, shall I?
(GEORGE *shows him into the hall. They get to the foot of the stairs, and the* MAN *turns*.)

MAN: (*officialdom relaxing*). You know, you people are a funny lot. I don't understand you. Look what you do to yourselves. And all for what? What do you get out of it? It beats me. Now take me and my wife. We don't have any worries. I've got my job during the day—secure, pension at the end of it. Mrs. Webb is at home, looking after the kiddies—she knows there'll be a pay-packet every Friday. And in the evenings, we sit at home together, or sometimes we'll go out. But we're happy. There's quite a lot to it, you know. (*Quite kindly*.) What could be better? I ask you? No, you think it over, son. You think it over.
(*He goes out of the front door.* JOSIE *comes downstairs in her dressing-gown*.)

JOSIE: (*quietly*). Ruth home yet?

GEORGE: No. Not yet.

JOSIE: Know where she is?

GEORGE: She's at the doctor's.

71

JOSIE: Doctor's? What for?

GEORGE: For me. (*Crossing to sitting-room.*)

JOSIE: For you? Thought you didn't believe in doctors.

GEORGE: (*turns*). I don't. She's picking something up for me.

JOSIE: (*going to him*). I should have thought you could have done that rather well yourself. What's she picking up for you?

GEORGE: What's called a report. You know? Making no progress, but he mustn't try so hard. Unpromising.

JOSIE: Oh, I see. (*Crossing through into kitchen.*) Think I'll have some hot milk.

(GEORGE *goes into the sitting-room after her, and picks up the scattered leaves of his manuscript.*)

PERCY: Well, young man—you're at it again I see.

GEORGE: Yes. I'm afraid I'm not getting very far with it though.

PERCY: I don't mean that. I mean you're busy fleecing money from someone else again.

GEORGE: What the hell are you talking about?

PERCY: Not content with taking the money we bring home, you're even trying to get hold of the money we pay in income tax. You're getting it all ways, aren't you, George?

GEORGE: I certainly am! Look here, Percy, you'd better be careful what you say——

PERCY: And I think you'd better be careful what *you* say. Telling a government official barefaced lies like that! That's a case—(*leaning forward with infinite relish*)— for the assizes, that is!

GEORGE: All right, I admit it. But Mrs. Elliot knows that she'll get back every penny, and more, for looking after me as she has.

PERCY: Accch! I don't believe it. Anyway, you don't think she'll be very pleased when she finds out where it comes from, do you? Assistance Board! To think of us having someone like that at the door. What'll people think of that? I know all about you my lad. I've checked up on you at my firm—you owe bills all over the place. Don't be surprised if you don't

72

have the police after you soon—for debt. *Debt!*
(*Thrilling with horror.*) Imagine that! Police coming
to my house—to me that's never owed a farthing to
anybody in all his life.

(*Doorbell rings, followed by violent knocking.*)

PERCY: And it wouldn't surprise me if that was them already.
I know a copper's knock when I hear it.

(*Exit quickly into kitchen.* GEORGE *sinks into arm-
chair, exhausted. Doorbell and knocking again. Pause.*
BARNEY EVANS *comes in through the front door. He is
wearing a rather old Crombie overcoat, an expensive
but crumpled suit, thick horn-rimmed glasses, and a
rakish brown Homburg hat. He is nearly fifty, and has
never had a doubt about anything in all that time.*)

BARNEY: Anyone there? Anyone at home? I say?

GEORGE: In here. Come in here.

BARNEY: Where? (*To sitting-room.*) In here? Oh yes. Good.
Sorry to butt in on you like this. The fact is——
(GEORGE *rises.*) Oh yes, you must be who I am looking
for.

GEORGE: Oh? Sit down, will you?

BARNEY: No, no, no—I can't stop a minute. I found I was
passing your door, so I thought I'd just pop in for a
few words. I haven't a London office any longer—
just for a moment, you see. I'm just on my way to
Brighton, as a matter of fact.

GEORGE: For the week-end?

BARNEY: Business and pleasure. (*Thoughtfully.*) Business—
mostly. Look, I'll come straight to the point, Mr.——

GEORGE: Dillon. George Dillon.

BARNEY: (*producing a script from his pocket*). Oh yes. It's on
here. George Dillon. Been in the business long?

GEORGE: Well—a few——

BARNEY: Thought so. Didn't ever play the Palace, Westport,
did you?

GEORGE: No, I didn't.

BARNEY: Face seemed familiar. Well, now—to get down to
it——

73

GEORGE: Is that my script you've got there?

BARNEY: That's right.

GEORGE: How on earth did you get hold of it?

BARNEY: Andy gave it to me.

GEORGE: Andy?

BARNEY: André Tetlock. You know him, don't you?

GEORGE: Oh—the Trident. Is he a friend of yours then?

BARNEY: Andy? I knew him when he was a chorus boy at the old Tivoli. You wouldn't remember that. Why, it was me put him back on his feet after that bit of trouble. You know that, don't you?

GEORGE: Yes?

BARNEY: He hadn't even got a set of underwear—I had to get that for him. Silly fellow! (*Sucks in his breath deprecatingly.*) Still, he's all right now. That was my idea—that bar, you know. Oh, he did it up himself, mind you—Andy's very clever with his hands. But it was my idea. And now that bar's packed every night. Can't get within a mile of the place. He doesn't have to worry whether he puts on a show or not. Get some odd types there, of course, but you know Andy—so everybody's happy. And as long as he can find enough authors willing to back their own plays with hard cash, *he* won't go without his bottle of gin, believe me. (*Produces a packet of cheroots.*) Got a match? I take it you *don't* have any capital of your own?

GEORGE: Right.

BARNEY: Yes, he said you'd told him you hadn't any money to put up yourself.

GEORGE: (*lighting his cheroot for him*). I rang him about it weeks ago. I remember he said he'd liked the play, but he'd passed it on to someone else.

BARNEY: Liked it! That's a good one. Andy doesn't *read* plays —he just puts 'em on. Provided of course he can make something out of it! Now, I've read this play of yours, and I'm interested. Are you willing to listen to a proposition?

74

GEORGE: Of course.

BARNEY: By the way, I'm Barney Evans. You've heard of me, of course?

(GEORGE *hesitates, but* BARNEY *doesn't wait.*)

Now, Andy's a friend of mine. I've done a lot for him—but he's only in the business in a very small way. Oh, he does himself all right. But it's small stuff. You wouldn't get anywhere much with him— You know that, of course?

GEORGE: Yes.

BARNEY: I'm only interested in the big money. Small stuff's not worth my while. I take it you *are* interested in money?

GEORGE: Is that a rhetorical question?

BARNEY: Eh?

GEORGE: Yes, I am.

BARNEY: That's all right then. I don't want to waste my time. This the first play you've written.

GEORGE: My seventh——

BARNEY: Dialogue's not bad, but these great long speeches— that's a mistake. People want action, excitement. I know—*you* think you're Bernard Shaw. But where's he today? Eh? People won't listen to him. Anyway, politics are out—you ought to know that. Now, take *My Skin is my Enemy!* I've got that on the road at the moment. That and *Slasher Girl!*

GEORGE: *My Skin is my*—— Oh yes, it's about the colour bar problem, isn't it?

BARNEY: Well, yes—but you see it's first-class entertainment! Played to £600 at Llandrindod Wells last week. Got the returns in my pocket now. It's controversial, I grant you, but it's the kind of thing people pay money to see. That's the kind of thing you want to write.

GEORGE: Still, I imagine you've got to be just a bit liberal-minded to back a play like that.

BARNEY: Eh?

GEORGE: I mean—putting on a play about coloured people.

BARNEY: Coloured people? I hate the bastards! You should

75

talk to the author about them. He can't even be civil to them. No—I know young fellows like you. You're interested in ideals still. Idealists. Don't think I don't know. I was an idealist myself once. I could tell you a lot, only I haven't got time now. But, make no mistake—ideals didn't get me where I am.

GEORGE: No?

BARNEY: You spend your time dabbling in politics, and vote in some ragged-arsed bunch of nobodies, who can't hardly pronounce the Queen's English properly, and where are you? Where are you? Nowhere. Crushed down in the mob, indistinguishable from the masses. What's the good of that to a young man with talent?

GEORGE: I should have thought you had a vested interest in the masses.

BARNEY: Most certainly. I admit it. And that's why I believe in education. Education—it always shows, and it always counts. That's why I say let them who've got it run the whole show. We're not going to get anywhere with these foreigners once they see they're no longer dealing with gentlemen. They're always impressed by an English gentleman. Just because they've got no breeding themselves, they know how to recognize it in others when they see it. Oh, yes. I could tell you a lot you don't know. However, I am diverting from what I came about.
(*He sprays his ash over the floor thoughtfully.*)
To get back to this play of yours. I think it's got possibilities, but it needs rewriting. Act One and Two won't be so bad, provided you cut out all the high-brow stuff, give it pace—you know: dirty it up a bit, you see.

GEORGE: I see.

BARNEY: Third Act's construction is weak. I could help you there—and I'd do it for quite a small consideration because I think you've got something. You know that's a very good idea—getting the girl in the family way.

GEORGE: You think so?

BARNEY: Never fails. Get someone in the family way in the Third Act—you're halfway there. I suppose you saw *I Was a Drug Fiend*?

GEORGE: No.

BARNEY: Didn't you really? No wonder you write like you do! I thought everyone had seen that! That was my show too. Why, we were playing to three and four thousand a week on the twice-nightly circuit with that. That's the sort of money you want to play to. Same thing in that: Third Act—girl's in the family way. Course, in that play, her elder sister goes out as a missionary and ends up dying upside down on an ant hill in her birthday suit. I spent six months in the South of France on what I made out of that show. (*Motor-horn toots outside.*) Here, I'll have to be going. As I say, you rewrite it as I tell you, maybe we can do business together and make some money for both of us. I'll read it through again, and drop you a line. In the meantime, I should redraft the whole thing, bearing in mind what I said. Right.

GEORGE: I'll have to think about it. The fact is—I'm not feeling up to much at the moment. I'm completely broke for one thing.

BARNEY: O.K. then. You'll be hearing from me. You take my advice—string along with me. I know this business inside and out. You forget about starving for Art's sake. That won't keep you alive five minutes. You've got to be ruthless. (*Moves into hall.*) Yes, there's no other word for it—absolutely ruthless. (GEORGE *follows him.*)

(BARNEY *picks up his hat from stand and knocks over the vase. He looks down at the pieces absent-mindedly.*)

BARNEY: Oh, sorry. Now you take Hitler—the greatest man that ever lived! Don't care what anyone says—you can't get away from it. He had the right idea, you've got to be ruthless, and it's the same in this business. Course he may have gone a bit too far sometimes.

GEORGE: Think so?

BARNEY: I do. I do think so, most definitely. Yes, he over-reached himself, no getting away from it. That's where all great men make their mistake—they over-reach themselves.

(*The car horn toots more insistently.*)

Hullo, blimey, she'll start smashing the windows in a minute. (GEORGE *follows him as he hurries to door.*) Well, you just remember what I said. Tell you what —I'll give you a ring on Monday. I'll be busy all the week-end. (*Opens door.*) By the way, that girl?

GEORGE: What girl?

BARNEY: The girl in your play—what do you call her?

GEORGE: Oh, you mean——

BARNEY: Build her up. Build her right up. She's—she's a prostitute *really* isn't she?

GEORGE: Well——

BARNEY: Of course she is! I've just had an idea—a new slant. Your title, what is it? (*He doesn't wait for a reply.*) Anyway, it won't bring anybody in. I've just thought of a smashing title. You know what we'll call it? "Telephone Tart", that's it! "Telephone Tart." You string along with me, George, I'll see you're all right. (*Exit.*)

(JOSIE *looks in from kitchen.*)

JOSIE: (*coming in with a glass of milk*). It's all right, he's gone. (*Sits in arm-chair.*) Don't know what all the fuss was about.

PERCY: Well, I hadn't shaved, you see. I should hate to let George down in front of his friends—what few he *has* got.

JOSIE: Oh, you are daft, Dad. You don't know what you're talking about half the time.

(GEORGE *comes slowly into sitting-room.*)

JOSIE: Who was it, George? Teddy-bear coat and all!

GEORGE: (*smiling wryly*). I suppose he's what you might call the poor man's Binkie.

JOSIE: What? Whatever's that? What's that, George?

78

(RUTH *comes in front door into sitting-room.*)

GEORGE: Oh, never mind. It doesn't really matter. Hello, Ruth.

RUTH: (*after a slight pause*). Hullo.

GEORGE: Well, did you go to the doctor's?

RUTH: Yes.

GEORGE: Well—(*laughing*)—don't stand there with the angel of death on your shoulder—what did he say?

RUTH: George—just come in here, will you, for a minute. (GEORGE *follows her into lounge.*)

JOSIE: Well, of all the—I like that, I must say! We're not good enough to know what's going on! (*Rising and going up to radiogram.*) I'm sure I don't want to hear what she got to say to George. Them and their secrets. (*She puts on Mambo record very loud.*) (JOSIE *then picks up a magazine and glances at it viciously, her foot wagging furiously. After a moment she gets up and goes over to the window and looks out in the same manner.* PERCY *watches her all the time. She catches him doing it.*)

JOSIE: Well, had your eyeful? (*She walks over-casually towards the lounge door.*) Real heart-to-heart they're having, aren't they? (*Over to mirror as* RUTH *comes out of the lounge and goes into the sitting-room and says something to* PERCY. MRS. ELLIOT *comes in at the front door, laden as usual. She goes into sitting-room and switches off the radiogram.*)

MRS. E.: Whatever do you want that thing on like that for, Josie? I could hear it halfway down the street. I thought you weren't well? (*Pause.*)

MRS. E.: Why, what is it? What's the matter with you all? What is it, Ruth?

PERCY: George has got T.B. (*In a voice like sandpaper.*)

MRS. E.: T.B., George. I don't believe it. It isn't true. There must be some mistake——

RUTH: There's no mistake. It's quite true, Kate. The doctor

79

will be coming up soon to let us know what the arrangements are.

MRS. E.: Does this mean that he'll have to go away?

(RUTH *nods her head.*)

George—poor old George. (*She moves into hall and up the stairs.*) George dear, where are you? He won't like this at all, will he? George——

(PERCY *comes out of room to foot of stairs as* MRS. E. *is halfway up.*)

PERCY: (*calling up loudly*). You'll have to burn everything, you know! All his sheets, blankets. Everything will have to be burnt, you know!

JOSIE: Oh, my God. Auntie Ruth! What's going to happen? What about me?

RUTH: You?

JOSIE: Yes, that's what I want to know—what's going to happen to me?

(QUICK CURTAIN)

ACT THREE

SCENE TWO

Winter. MRS. ELLIOT *is on stage alone. She is looking up the stairs.* GEORGE'S *hat, coat and suitcase are standing in the hall. She is looking very anxious. She picks up the hat and coat, and hangs them up carefully on the hallstand. Then she goes back to the sitting-room. She goes over to the wedding group picture, and stares up at it. As she is doing this* PERCY *comes in at the front door. He takes off his hat and coat, hangs them up beside* GEORGE'S, *and comes into the sitting-room.*

PERCY: So he's back then?

MRS. E.: Yes.

PERCY: Where is he?

MRS. E.: Upstairs—talking to Josie.

PERCY: Upstairs?

MRS. E.: Yes. She wasn't feeling too good this morning, so I told her to stay in bed. I didn't want to take any chances. I think she was over-excited at the thought of George coming back.

PERCY: Excited, was she?

MRS. E.: Of course she was. She's thought about nothing else for weeks.

PERCY: Well, well! She's in for a bit of a shock, isn't she?

MRS. E.: Listen to me, Percy. I've told you—you're to keep out of this. It's nothing to do with you. The only two people it need concern at the moment are George and myself. Above all, I don't want one word of this to get to Josie's ears. We've no idea what might happen if she was to get a shock like that. And in her present condition. If you so much as open your mouth about it to her—you can pack your bags and go. You

F   81

understand? Besides, we don't know yet that it's true
—not for certain. We've only got your word for it,
and we all know what a nasty mind you've got. It
would please you to think something rotten of
George. You've always been against him. You're
jealous of him—that's why.

PERCY: Me? Jealous of him! That wreck!

MRS. E.: He's a gentleman—which is something you'll never
be.

PERCY: Oh, he is, is he? Perhaps that's why he can't even
earn the price of a cup of tea!

MRS. E.: That's all *you* know.

PERCY: And what does that mean, exactly?

MRS. E.: Never you mind. But there's a lot you don't know
about George. George will come out tops in the end
—you wait.

PERCY: Seems more like there was a lot *all* of us didn't know
about him.

MRS. E.: You don't understand, Percy. And what's more, you
never will. You think everyone's like yourself. George
is an artist——

PERCY: And what's *that* supposed to mean?

MRS. E.: He's sensitive, proud—he suffers deeply. Raymond
was like that—you never liked him, and he was your
own son. That boy's gone through a lot—he doesn't
have to tell me that. I could tell the first time I ever
spoke to him. I knew he was a good fellow, that all
he wanted was a chance to bring a little pleasure to
other people. I don't think that's so much of a crime,
anyway. Oh, he's never said anything to me, but I've
known what he's been going through all these months.
When he's come back here in the evenings, when he
couldn't get a job or any kind of encouragement at
all, when people like you were sneering at him, and
nobody wanted him. He didn't think I knew when he
was feeling sick with disappointment. He didn't think
I knew he was trying to pass it off, by making us
laugh, and pretending that everything was going to

82

be all right. And I've never been able to tell him because I can't express myself properly—not like he can. He's got a gift for it—that's why he's an artist. That's why he's different from us. But he'll have his own way, in the end, you mark my words. He'll show them all—and you. God always pays debts without money. I've got down on my knees at night, and prayed for that boy. I've prayed that he'll be well, and get on, and be happy—here—with us.

PERCY: With us?

MRS. E.: If that's what he wants. And I believe it is. I know we're not the kind of people George is used to, and probably likes being with—he must have felt it sometimes. Not that he's ever said anything—he's too well brought up for that. He just accepts us for what we are. He's settled in here. And while he's been in that hospital all these weeks, he's known he's got somewhere to come back to. He's known that somebody wants him, anyway, and that's a great deal when you're laying there in bed, and you don't know properly whether you're going to live or die. To know that someone is counting the days until you come home.

PERCY: What's he look like?

MRS. E.: A bit thin. But who wouldn't look thin on that hospital food? I'll soon feed him up.

PERCY: Did you manage to have a word with the doctor?

MRS. E.: No, I didn't.

PERCY: Well, why not?

MRS. E.: Because I wasn't going to ask the doctor a lot of questions behind George's back, that's why. He's back—that's all I care about, that's all I want to know at the moment. Things will work themselves out somehow. George won't let us down.

PERCY: Well, we shall soon see, shan't we? He's a long time up there, don't you think? And what's he going to do about his wife?

MRS. E.: How do I know what he's going to do? Why can't

83

you shut up about it! You've talked about nothing
else for days now.

PERCY: You mean to say you didn't tackle him about it?

MRS. E.: I didn't have an opportunity. I couldn't bring it up
on the bus, could I? Besides, I couldn't start on him
straight away. And as soon as we got back, he wanted
to go up and see Josie, naturally.

PERCY: Well, you wait till he comes down. If you're afraid
to tackle him about it, I'm not.

MRS. E.: I meant what I said, you know. If you try and cause
trouble in this house, you can go.

PERCY: I think it's disgusting. Carrying on in someone else's
house—a married man at that! Do you know what?
It's my belief that there was something between him
and your sister Ruth—and that's why she decided to
pack her bags, and go, all of a sudden.

MRS. E.: Oh, don't be so childish, for heaven's sake, Percy.
You've got sex on the brain. I must admit you could
have knocked me down when Ruth told me she was
going to find herself a room somewhere. I mean—it
seemed a bit suspicious. She didn't even give a proper
explanation. Just said that she felt she had to "get
out of it". It seemed a funny thing to say, and
especially after all these years. Of course, she always
was a dark horse. But, as for her and George—it's
ridiculous. Why, she's old enough to be his
mother. *Now Stop talking about it & help me make up the fire*

PERCY: (*as he goes to lounge*). Oh, you women—you go
on and on.

(RUTH *appears at front door—unlocking it enters,
leaving door open.*)

(RUTH *enters sitting-room.*)

RUTH: (*quietly*). Kate. Kate. *Kitchen*

(GEORGE *comes downstairs—shuts front door. Then
goes towards sitting-room—meets* RUTH *face to face
in the doorway.*)

RUTH: Hello George. Are you better?

GEORGE: You're not really going, are you?

84

RUTH: I was coming to collect my things this morning—but I couldn't.

GEORGE: In fact it's quite a coincidence meeting you.

RUTH: No. Not really. I suppose it was silly of me to come when I knew you'd be back. I always seem to let myself in for farewells.

GEORGE: We both ought to be pretty good at them by now. (*Pause.*) Are you really leaving then?

RUTH: Not again, please. There's only a few minutes.

GEORGE: (*very quietly*). What's going to happen to me?

RUTH: George—don't! Try and help a little. (*Pause.*)

GEORGE: Isn't it hell—loving people?

RUTH: Yes—hell.

GEORGE: Still sounds rather feeble when you say it though. Rather like "shift me—I'm burning". What are you going to do?

RUTH: I don't know. Maybe find some scruffy wretch with a thumb-nail sketch of a talent, and spend my time emptying bits of brown cigarette stubs from his saucer —generally cleaning up.

GEORGE: Did you ever look up your—friend? (*He lifts up the wrist-watch.*)

RUTH: Yes. I did. Soon after you came in here. But he wasn't at the same place any more. His landlord gave me his new address. Number something Eaton Square.

GEORGE: But of course, my dear—everyone lives in Eaton Square.

RUTH: Apparently, she's in publishing. She's just published his book last week. But I mustn't be unfair—she didn't write the reviews as well. They fairly raved. He's on top of the world.

GEORGE: You know I've been waiting for you to tell me that you're old enough to be my mother. Still, mothers don't walk out on their sons—or do they?

RUTH: How's Josie—have you seen her yet?

GEORGE: God! What a farce! What pure, screaming farce!

85

(*He starts to laugh.*)

RUTH: For heaven's sake!

GEORGE: Sorry. I just thought of something. How to make
sure of your Third Act. Never fails! (*Roars with
laughter.*) Never fails! (*Subsides almost immediately.*)
Don't panic. I'll not get maudlin. I probably would
start howling any minute, only I'm afraid of getting
the bird from my best audience.
(*He looks away from her, and adds in a strangled
voice, barely audible.*)
Don't leave me on my own!
(*But he turns back quickly.*)
You haven't mentioned my—success—once.

RUTH: I didn't know whether you expected me to
congratulate you or not.

GEORGE: Second week of tour—I've got the returns here. Look:
Empire Theatre, Llandrindod Wells—week's gross
takings £647 18s. 4d. Long-hair drama gets a haircut
from Mr. Barney Evans!

RUTH: I simply can't bear to go on watching you any longer.

GEORGE: But don't you think it's all very comic? I seem to
remember some famous comedian saying once that
he'd never seen anything funny that wasn't terrible.
So don't think I'll mind if you laugh. I expect it. We
should be both good for a titter, anyway. That's why
religion is so damned deadly—it's not even good for
a giggle. And what's life without a good giggle, eh?
That's what I always say! Isn't that what you always
say, Ruth?

RUTH: Let go of my hand. You're hurting me.

GEORGE: Well—isn't it? No. Perhaps it isn't. We never really
had the same sense of humour, after all.

RUTH: Please don't try to hurt yourself any more by trying to
hit back at me. I know how you feel. You're overcome
with failure. Eternal bloody failure.

GEORGE: But I'm not a failure, I'm a—success.

RUTH: Are you, George? (*She turns away.*)

GEORGE: Listen! I'll make you laugh yet, before you go. Just

86

a trip on the stage-cloth, and Lear teeters on, his crown round his ears, his grubby tights full of moth-holes. How they all long for those tights to fall down. What a relief it would be! Oh, we should all use stronger elastic. And the less sure we are of our pathetic little divine rights, the stronger the elastic we should use. You've seen the whole, shabby, solemn pretence now. This is where you came in. For God's sake go.

(*She turns to go.*)

GEORGE: No, wait. Shall I recite my epitaph to you? Yes, do recite your epitaph to me. "Here lies the body of George Dillon, aged thirty-four—or thereabouts—who thought, who hoped, he was that mysterious, ridiculous being called an artist. He never allowed himself one day of peace. He worshipped the physical things of this world, and was betrayed by his own body. He loved also the things of the mind, but his own brain was a cripple from the waist down. He achieved nothing he set out to do. He made no one happy, no one look up with excitement when he entered the room. He was always troubled with wind round his heart, but he loved no one successfully. He was a bit of a bore, and, frankly, rather useless. But the germs loved him. (*He doesn't see* RUTH *as she goes out and up the stairs*.) Even his sentimental epitaph is probably a pastiche of someone or other, but he doesn't quite know who. And, in the end, it doesn't really matter. (*He turns, but* RUTH *has gone*.)

(*Bell rings,* PERCY *opens door*.)

NORAH: (*coming in*). Only me. Forgot my key again. Is George back yet? (*Into room*). George! You are back!

GEORGE: Yes, Norah, I'm back again, with a face like the death of kings.

NORAH: (*rushes to him*). Oh, George, you look fine! Doesn't he, Dad? I thought you'd look awful—but you look fine. (*Kisses him as* MRS. E. *comes in from kitchen*.)

GEORGE: Here—mind my ribs!

NORAH: Oh, we'll soon feed you up, won't we, Mum?
(*She takes him into the sitting-room*, PERCY *follows*.)
MRS. E.: We certainly will. We're going to look after him
from now on. He can sit in here all day and rest,
and—keep himself happy. Can't you, George?
GEORGE: Rather.
MRS. E.: He can lie down on the settee in the afternoons with
his books and things, and—oh, I forgot! We got you
a little homecoming present, didn't we, Norah?
NORAH: Shall I go up and get it?
MRS. E.: If you like, dear, I don't know whether George feels
up to opening presents. He must feel all in after that
journey. I expect he'd like a bit of a rest.
GEORGE: I'm all right. I'd like a cup of tea though.
MRS. E.: It's all ready. And I'll get you something to eat in no
time.
NORAH: All right, then. I'll go and get it. I'll just pop in and
have a look at Josie. Have you seen her, George?
MRS. E.: He's been in there ever since he came in, haven't
you, George?
NORAH: (*crossing to and up stairs*). She's been so excited at the
thought of you coming back. She's talked about
nothing else for days. (*She laughs*.) Isn't love grand!
(*Exit*.)
MRS. E.: It's true, George. She's been quite a changed girl
since you went away. I'm afraid she did used to be a
bit on the lazy side sometimes, but not now—you
wouldn't know her. Why, Sunday we spent practically
all evening getting your room ready and looking nice.
And Norah's been the same. Why, she's even booked
seats for a coach ride for all of us down to the seaside.
PERCY: Well? How are you feeling, George?
GEORGE: Sorry, Percy. I haven't had a chance to say hullo yet,
have I? (*Offers his hand*.)
PERCY: (*shakes perfunctorily*). How have they been treating
you?
GEORGE: Oh, not too bad, thanks. But it's certainly good to be
back. You've all given me such a welcome.

88

PERCY: It's quite a nice place down there, I believe.

GEORGE: It's all right.

PERCY: Nice country.

GEORGE: Oh, lovely.

PERCY: Isn't that near Tunbridge Wells?

GEORGE: Not far.

MRS. E.: I don't suppose he wants to talk much now, Percy. Let him have a rest first. He's tired.

PERCY. They say that's a nice town.

GEORGE: It's pleasant enough.

PERCY: Ever been there, George?

GEORGE: What are you getting at?

PERCY: I think you *know* what I'm getting at.

GEORGE: (*to* MRS. E.). What is it? You're upset about something, aren't you. I could tell something was wrong when you met me at the hospital. And all the way home on the bus.

PERCY: I suppose you didn't happen to be in Tunbridge Wells on June 22nd, 1943, did you?
(*Pause.*)

GEORGE: I see.

MRS. E.: George—it's not true, is it? I was sure he'd made a mistake.

GEORGE: No, He hasn't made a mistake. I *was* married in Tunbridge Wells, and it was in 1943. The middle of June. It poured with rain. How did you find out?

PERCY: Through my firm, as a matter of fact. As you know, it's our job to check on people's credentials, etc., for hire purchase firms and the like. Well, last week, I found myself checking on a certain Ann Scott, on behalf of a building society. She's contemplating buying some big property in Chelsea. Good report— excellent banker's references and all that. Living in large house in upper class district. And it seems her married name is Mrs. George Dillon. Well? What have you got to say?

GEORGE: Well?

MRS. E.: Oh, dear.

GEORGE: What do you want me to say?

MRS. E.: I don't know, George. I'm so upset, I don't know where I am. I suppose it's not your fault, but——

GEORGE: But, my dear, I don't see what there is to be so upset about. This doesn't change anything.

MRS. E.: But—but what about Josie?

GEORGE: Nothing is changed, I tell you. It's simply that neither my wife nor I have ever bothered about a divorce. She's had other things to think about, and I've never had the money. But it's all easily settled. There's nothing to worry about. I promise you.

MRS. E.: You're not just saying this, George? I'd rather——

GEORGE: Of course not. I've come home, haven't I?

MRS. E.: Yes, you have. You've come home, thank heaven.

GEORGE: You see, my wife never was anything. With Josie, it's different. I know exactly where I am.

MRS. E.: She loves you, George. She really does.

GEORGE: Yes. I know.

PERCY: It said on my report that she's an actress, this wife of yours.

(PERCY *feels cheated, and is desperately looking round for something else.*)

GEORGE: Right.

PERCY: She must do pretty well at it then.

GEORGE: She does.

PERCY: Can't say I've ever heard the name.

GEORGE: On the contrary, you know her very well.

PERCY: What do you mean?

GEORGE: I mean that somebody must have slipped up rather badly in your report. They seem to have left out her stage name.

PERCY: Stage name?

GEORGE: We both thought "Ann Scott" a bit commonplace.

PERCY: Who is she then?

GEORGE: Well, you've always told me that she's the only one in your favourite television parlour game who's really any good at all. In fact, you've said so many times.

PERCY: You don't mean—— What? Not *her*!

90

GEORGE: Her.

PERCY: Well, I'll be . . .

GEORGE: Yes. It's always puzzled me why you should admire her so much. Or anyone else for that matter.

MRS. E.: But George—honestly, I don't know where I am. Now that—well—now that you're a success, how do you know that your wife won't want you back?

GEORGE: Somehow, I don't think that will influence her!

PERCY: What are you talking about? Now that he's a success?

MRS. E.: (*recovered and triumphant*). Well, I don't see why he shouldn't know now, do you, George?

GEORGE: No, I don't see why not.

MRS. E.: George has had his play put on. It's on tour at the moment, and last week it made—tell him how much it made, George.

GEORGE: £647 18s. 4d. (*Flourishing returns.*)

MRS. E.: And he gets five per cent of that every week, so perhaps that will shut you up a bit.

PERCY: (*staring at returns*). Well! Fancy that! Why didn't somebody tell me?

MRS. E.: Why should they? Well, I mustn't stand here wasting time. You must be hungry, George.
(*Phone rings.*)

MRS. E.: Do answer that, Percy, will you? Wish Norah would hurry up.
(PERCY *goes to phone.* NORAH *comes down stairs carrying parcel into sitting-room.*)

NORAH: Josie says she won't be long, she's going to get up.

PERCY: What's that? Oh, yes, hang on a minute while I find my pencil. All right—go ahead.

NORAH: Well, George, here we are—I can't wait to see his face when he opens it, Mum.

GEORGE: Well——

MRS. E.: No, wait till Josie comes down. She'll want to be with him when he opens it.

NORAH: Oh, blow that. She's got all the time in the world with him now. If he won't open it, I will.

91

PERCY: Yes. Yes. I've got that. Who? What? What name? Right. Good-bye.

MRS. E.: All right then. I don't suppose she'll mind. Go on, George, open it.

(GEORGE *starts opening the parcel.*)

PERCY: (*coming in*). That was for you, George. A telegram.

GEORGE: Oh, who from?

PERCY: Somebody called Barney. I've got it written down here.

GEORGE: Read it out, will you? I'm busy at the moment.

PERCY: It says "Playing capacity business. May this be the first of many smash hits together. Welcome home—Barney."

MRS. E.: Well, wasn't that nice of him?

GEORGE: Yes, good old Barney. Now, what have we here? (*Stands back to reveal a portable typewriter.*) Well! Look at that!

MRS. E.: I hope you like it, George.

GEORGE: Like it! I should think I do! I think it must be the nicest present I've had. What can I say? (*He kisses them both.*) Thank you both. Thank you for everything.

MRS. E.: That's all right, George. Believe me, all my prayers have been answered. Mr. Colwyn-Stuart prayed for you too, every week you were away. All I want is for us all to be happy. Come along now, sit down, while I get the supper. Give him a chair, Percy, you look all in, dear.

PERCY: Oh, sorry. Here you are.

NORAH: It'll be nice, having George for a brother-in-law.

GEORGE: Yes, of course it will, Norah. It's about time you got married yourself, isn't it?

MRS. E.: She almost has been——

NORAH: —Twice.

GEORGE: I'm sorry.

MRS. E.: The last one was an American.

NORAH: Yes. The last time I saw him, we were going to get a bus to Richmond. He just simply said suddenly:

"Well, so long, honey, it's been nice knowing you"
and got on a bus going in the opposite direction. It's
swimming on the telly tonight. I think I'll go and
watch it, if you'll excuse me.
(*She goes into lounge. Slight pause.*)

MRS. E.: Well, I don't know. What with one thing and
another! That's right, George, dear. Just you relax
from now on. And you let him alone, Percy. I've
always believed in you, George. Always. I knew he'd
come out tops.
(MRS. ELLIOT *goes into kitchen.* GEORGE *leans back,
tired.* PERCY *turns on radio. Jazz—"If you can't give
me a dollar, give me a lousy dime.*")

PERCY: Not too loud for you, George?

GEORGE: No—fine. (*Pause.*)

PERCY: I can't get over it you know.

GEORGE: What?

PERCY: Your wife, I mean. Big star like that. Surprised she
couldn't have helped you on a bit all this time. Still,
you're doing all right yourself now, by the look of it.
Turned out to be Bernard Shaw, after all, eh? I
suppose you'll be writing some more plays when you
start feeling better again?

GEORGE: I dare say.

PERCY: I see. Same sort of thing?
(RUTH *comes down slowly with suitcase.*)

GEORGE: Yes. Same sort of thing.

PERCY: Well, that's good, isn't it? What was the name of
that theatre again?

GEORGE: The Empire Theatre, Llandrindod Wells.
(*The sound of* JOSIE'S *voice singing comes from upstairs.
From the lounge, the telly is playing music.*)

PERCY: Well, I don't think it would do any harm if we all
have a little drink on this. (*To cocktail cabinet.*) If
we're going to start living in style, we may as well get
into the way of using this, eh?
(*He opens the cocktail cabinet, revealing all its hidden
glory.* RUTH *exits through front door.*)

93

PERCY: Now, where are we. (*Staring into cabinet.*)

MRS. E.: That's right. Let's have a little drink.

GEORGE: (*in a flat, empty voice*). Yes, let's have a little drink—to celebrate.

PERCY: Music too, would not be inappropriate. (*Putting on record.*)

GEORGE: Music too, would not be inappropriate.
(JOSIE *sings, off.*)

PERCY: Well, we can't leave the blushing bride upstairs all on her own, can we? I'll give her a yell, shall I, George?
(*He goes out, calling upstairs,* GEORGE *goes to the door. He looks trapped and looks around the room and the objects in it; he notices the birds on the wall.*)

GEORGE: Those bloody birds!
(*Enter* MRS. ELLIOT. *He stares at her as if for the first time, then his face breaks into a mechanical smile.*)
Come on, Mum, let's dance!
(*They dance together for a few moments.*)

(SLOW CURTAIN)

94

Act II

Lighten it much more,

again in after kaput.

Watch. staccato.

Kiss ungainly.

New scene, "Blimey those birds."

enthusiasm for cocktail cabinet.

get to George quicker. "Yes you are
        a character"

lift, "How pompous can you get"

Barnum + Bailey definite song.

Words in duel.

over your own
Conscious of the story & interest audience

Too quiet. (quicker.)
Lighter out. (practise)

Laugh, better.

frustrated anger more often.

Read play again as a story,

X feed each other emotionally X

change "agonizing bubbles of personality".

Start growing "How pompous".

"Let me go" good but of the throat.

Act IV + III

party secretary stressing.

close . kitchen door..

upstage projection

caustic = "parts you play."

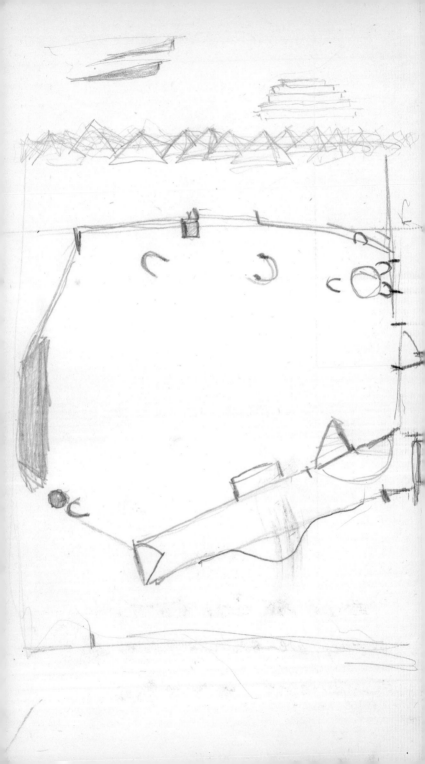